THE ICONOCLAST'S
GUIDE TO
MUSIC

DOG 'n' BONE

THE ICONOCLAST'S

— GUIDE TO —

MUSIC

UNRAVELING THE MINDSET
OF A MUSIC SNOB IN
50 DIGESTIBLE CHUNKS

STEVE JELBERT
with illustrations by Lord Dunsby

DOG 'n' BONE

For Kate, who has to listen to this stuff in real time
Dedicated to my mother, who loved music, and my father, who was
suspicious of it.

Published in 2013 by Dog 'n' Bone Books
An imprint of Ryland Peters & Small Ltd
20–21 Jockey's Fields   519 Broadway, 5th Floor
London WC1R 4BW   New York, NY 10012
www.dogandbonebooks.com

10 9 8 7 6 5 4 3 2 1

Text © Steve Jelbert 2013
Design and illustration © Dog 'n' Bone Books 2013

A CIP catalog record for this book is available from the Library of Congress and the
British Library.

ISBN: 978 1 909313 02 6

Printed in China
Editor: Caroline West
Design: Wide Open Design
Illustration: Steve Millington aka Lord Dunsby

For digital editions, visit www.cicobooks.com/apps.php

Contents

Introduction

If someone should announce that they don't like coffee or chocolate or, God forbid, potatoes, you might disagree but you wouldn't question their sanity. But if a stranger declares that they don't like music, you'd think them rather weird. For music is what separates us from the animals (except for whales and birds) and makes us human. It marks an entire area of human endeavor—whale song is for a strictly limited market (whales). Birds like to sing, true, but even the keenest avian performers have a limited range of subjects, such as "will you be my bird?" and "over here there are worms!" Human beings can propose procreation through song, and then bewail its lack. They can use it to boast about their possessions, be they tangible and material—such as an automobile or a large piece of jewelry—or less solid and more of an abstract concept—like the taste of Cristal champagne or a national anthem. You can tell a story, or simply express emotion, or even just knock up a good beat for moving to.

And like a fist in the guts or a dog bite, music is universally understood. Literally, in many cases, for keyboards and other instruments are identical in layout, whatever music they produce. No wonder Chinese power ballads are just as terrible as the power ballads of, say, Celine Dion, a French-speaking Canadian singer popular with English-speaking audiences, who once won the Eurovision Song Contest, representing Switzerland, a country where most people speak German (but can get by in French and Italian; and English).

Written music, like chemical equations and text emoticons, is an internationally understood language. But even those of us who don't read it—me, Sir Paul McCartney, Stevie Wonder—can, and do, respond to the emotional impact of melody and rhythm; even those beyond the familiar western twelve-note scale or in wholly unfamiliar tongues. For all we know, those exotic sounds could be advertising jingles for personal hygiene products but, by reacting to them emotionally, anyone can find meaning. Incidentally, this is a strong argument for never listening to lyrics, possibly an even stronger one than the dreadful quality of most lyrics.

So treat this little book as a music guide for non-humans, aliens from another world maybe. Inside you'll find answers to some questions no one could previously be bothered to ask about.

"IT ALWAYS STARTS WITH FLUTES FOR SOME REASON, FROM EGYPT TO INDIA, CHINA, AND BEYOND"
Valorie Salimpoor

Chapter 1
Music—
How Is It Made?

With the Voice

It all starts with the voice. Once early humans realized that their vocal cords could be used for purposes other than scaring away animals and warning their offspring not to touch fire, a whole new expressive language came into being. No longer was a club or similar weapon needed to seduce a prospective breeding partner. Instead, a chap could display his manly prowess by grunting in a rhythmic and melodic pattern. (This would reach its apotheosis toward the end of the 20th century when soul singer Alexander O'Neal installed a super-kingsize bed on stage while performing, thus confirming his alpha-male status and giving him his pick of the female members in the audience.)

Early woman could also use this newly found skill to ensnare a man (or put him off if she preferred—a technique later perfected by Yoko Ono and Courtney Love). This meant a significant shift in the traditional battle of the sexes. If man wanted to hear that sweet, sweet feminine voice, then he had better buck up his ideas and be nice. Indeed, it's entirely possible (though unlikely) that high-heeled shoes were invented by early man as a way of inducing involuntary yelps, which could be mistaken for mating cries in early woman.

In short, the vocal cords or folds (two mucous membranes stretched across the larynx) vibrate as air is forced across them, producing sound which can be altered in pitch and power. The tongue and mouth have a part to play in modifying this sound and creating language, but we all know that the most expressive singers can reduce a listener to tears with wordless vocals alone—certainly, I've wept when Van Morrison has turned up to ruin a perfectly good festival bill.

The possessors of such voices soon learnt that they could use their ability to their own advantage. When God was invented a few thousand years ago, singers could hold down a steady job frightening the populace on His behalf. In ancient Greece, the chorus was created as a way of employing less talented vocalists. Medieval troubadours used their gift to charm wealthy women, sometimes with fatal consequences. Ballad singers in early modern England started a tradition of singing the news, which later transferred to North America where a young Bob Dylan perfected it right up to the point where he became the news and got all coy about mentioning Bob Dylan in his songs. The theme is clear nonetheless: we all remember the singer.

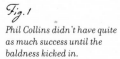

Fig. 1

Phil Collins didn't have quite as much success until the baldness kicked in.

With Technology

Technology has always led music rather than the other way round. Even simple descriptive names such as the pianoforte ("soft-loud" in Italian) make it clear what the instrument can 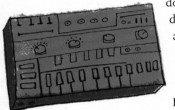 do, a tradition continued by the double bass, the Emulator synth, and the wah-wah pedal. From Bach's *The Well-Tempered Clavier* (1722) to *Sparky's Magic Piano* (1948) and the Crazy Frog (2003), the sound has influenced the music being made. It was the electric guitar that invented the guitar hero. It might have been invented to make the rhythm guitar audible in the big bands, but from Charlie Christian onward, via bluesmen like B.B. King, Albert King, and Freddie King, it makes a perfect monophonic solo instrument.

Of equal importance was the discovery that abusing technology was just as likely to produce something good. From Link Wray and Dave Davies playing through broken amplifiers, thus adding glorious fuzz guitar to the basic palette of pop music, to East End teenagers fascinated with samplers that sped up rhythms without altering their pitch (the basic building block of drum 'n' bass), throwing away the manual can be an artistically liberating action. Whacking up the Auto-Tune created a new way to annoy the listeners from a program originally intended to spare their ears the pain of hearing an off-pitch singer.

So many instruments have been invented to do a particular job that we've forgotten what they were invented for in the first place. The rotating Leslie speaker, the familiar wobbly sound of energetic jazz players like Jimmy Smith, was intended to replicate a church pipe organ, but became popular for its own virtues, especially while psychedelia and its narcotics were fashionable. Adolphe Sax intended his saxophone to fill the volume gap between woodwind and brass, not to signify "cool" in clichéd advertising. Most famously, the Vocoder started out as a military tool to encode voice transmissions before its robotic tones became the signature sound of over-produced seventies' pop records.

Yet technology often works best when it's only partly perfected. Was ska really invented because Jamaicans couldn't get a clear signal when listening to American stations broadcasting fifties' New Orleans r 'n' b, instead hearing it washing back and forth in regular time? Aren't songs like *Tomorrow Never Knows* (The Beatles) or *How Soon Is Now* (The Smiths) all the better for being unrepeatable performances that used manual technology? Having the idea is the most important thing, even if it's the device that inspires it.

With Instruments

Making music isn't just about the idea. How you transmit that idea is equally important, and though a touchscreen tablet might do at pinch, ultimately it won't impress your parents much. There are many physical methods of extracting sound, from the elemental—percussion, boogie-woogie piano—to the less than obvious, which usually involve blistered lips. But all of them require skill, patience, imagination, and, frankly, a suspension of disbelief.

THINGS YOU HIT

The voice is a great thing, but it's not particularly easy to dance to. In fact, it took several millennia for its percussive qualities to be recognized, when urban youth too poor to own a drum machine took up "beat boxing," a primitive form of homemade cyborging, which saw participants attempt to impersonate an electronic noise generator. (Early electro was big on the old robot/human interface—producer Curtis Mantronik, born Kurtis El Khaleel, ditched a perfectly good pop name to sound more man-machiney.)

It remains a useful way for those with less, er, musical voices to take part. But better still is hitting something with something else in regular time—maybe the leg bone of a saber-toothed lion on an echoey slab of lava. If you can get a bit of swing into it, then all the better. Cave paintings that appear to show groups of Neanderthals getting down to "The One" have changed academic theories about the invention of funk (though the stick men may just have been celebrating the death of a mammoth).

Obviously, just about anything can be hit to produce a sound, if not necessarily a musical one, from sheet metal to a side of beef. Pianos and guitars often sound better if assaulted by the unwitting and hopeless—few things delight more than the sight of a cat scaring itself by wandering across a keyboard. Drums should be scary. Their original function was to provide a terrifying soundtrack when two tribes went to war. The walls of the city didn't fall to the descant recorder, that's for sure.

Today musicians carry on this martial tradition by using double or even triple beaters to hit their bass drums, proving that sonic warfare can be conducted even when sitting down. Even the rhythmic markers of electronic music can prove unexpectedly violent, as anyone who's ever heard a

Fig. 2

Come down to Castro's this Saturday.
Our resident DJ High Fidelity will be playing
all the latest disco hits to make you groove.

car alarm set off by the sub-bass seeping from a tired old Beemer can testify.

Percussion isn't all about death and destruction, of course, though a near apocalypse altered the course of dance music. If Fidel Castro hadn't annoyed the United States into a trade embargo by hosting Soviet nuclear missiles in 1962, then New Yorker Martin Cohen would have been able to buy Cuban instruments instead of founding Latin Percussion and making his own bongos and beyond— and so crucially influencing the sound of disco. Where would disco music have even been without the plastic wood block? From such seemingly unconnected events, musical innovation is forged.

THINGS WITH STRINGS

If you want to be flash, you play something with strings. The piano might be versatile and a sax might look cool, but from Paganini, via Robert Johnson, to Jimmy Page, the only musicians that get accused of reaching a pact with the Devil (the actual devil out of the Bible and that, not a major label) are strumming or bowing something with at least four strings. (Page would revolutionize guitar-playing by using a violin bow to distract the audience during the duller bits of *Dazed and Confused*. And Paganini, a tidy guitarist, would have surely thrust his crotch against a Marshall stack if it had been invented, being a noted show-off.)

There's just something satisfying about the widely spread family of string instruments. From stand-up double bass to delicate cello, from the bluegrass banjo to windmilling on an electric guitar, all the best bits of music involve a bit of catgut or wire resonating through a soundbox or into an electric pick-up.

With only a few small exceptions (it's not the easiest task to exude sex appeal whilst strumming a harp), nearly all string instruments are easy to pose with while walking around the stage and winking at the cuter members of the audience. And, while smashing up a piano requires additional tools such as a sledgehammer, any angry axman or furious fiddler can express themselves through solo destruction.

I'm biased, obviously, but the electric guitar has actually been perfected. The Fender Stratocaster, introduced in 1954, manages to combine space-age fantasy with perfect function. It should be like driving around in the Batmobile or wearing golf shirts non-ironically—Fender would paint it in any DuPont car color the buyer fancied. But it remains iconic, and not only through the obvious associations with those who famously played it: Buddy Holly, Hank Marvin, Jimi Hendrix (a fan of American mass-production), Nile Rodgers (who labeled his "The Hitmaker"), and every other guitarist ever.

Strats can be repaired easily after a fit of exhibitionism. When luthiers started to design extreme metal guitars for extreme metal players, the flat Strat was the basic template, rather than the Gibson Les Paul with its traditional arched top. Because it works and it's been around so long, it just looks like a guitar rather than someone's idea of the future, but that's what it is. No wonder it's just one letter away from a Strad, another perfect stringed instrument.

THINGS YOU FORCE AIR THROUGH

The flute was the earliest instrument invented by man, though presumably it was fashioned   by a bored cave-dweller from an animal bone into some kind of primitive, non-vegetarian recorder rather than the metal tube wielded to such effect by the likes of twinkly Irishman James Galway, one-legged rock singer Jethro Tull, and Ron Burgundy in the movie *Anchorman*. There is something elemental about sticking something in your mouth and blowing. It's no wonder that the French expression *faire une pipe* should be so, er, déclassé. (You can, I'm sure, work it out.)

But the flute was only the start. Wind instruments range from the melodica, a hand-held keyboard powered by air and beloved of reggae musicians, to the Aeolian harp, which is, that in fact, a string instrument which produces sound when the wind blows through it. The woodwinds, especially reed instruments such as the bassoon, clarinet, and oboe, all produce sounds as reassuring as a sleeping baby breathing. Brass includes trumpets, tubas, lovely trombones, and the French horn, mysteriously also known as the cor anglais or "English horn." And let's not forget the vuvuzela, a traditional South African instrument made of traditional Chinese plastic and capable of producing up to two different notes, both of which dominated the crowd noise at

2010's soccer World Cup. Incidentally, musicologists define brass instruments as those that use the lips to create sound, which means that the didgeridoo counts as brass, though it's rarely seen in works' brass bands. The saxophone, though actually made of brass, is a woodwind instrument because it utilizes a reed.

Other wind-powered instruments of torture, such as the accordion, the deathly harmonium, and the concertina can at least be played while their operator sings to cover up the noise. Few instruments have inspired a joke as good as the venerable one-liner: "a gentleman is someone who knows how to play the accordion, but does not." Most controversially, the continuing debate about Scottish independence means that the bagpipes, sometimes known as "the infernal Tartan noise bag" are likely to remain a divisive issue, not least among Scots in favor of independence but opposed to the inevitable explosion of bagpipery that will doubtless accompany independence celebrations. No wonder they've long been associated with the military, presumably to drive soldiers into a state of murderous fury.

THINGS YOU TINKLE

Just like the typewriter layout, the piano keyboard has become a universal standard. And, just like the typewriter layout, it's not perfect but we're all stuck with it anyway and it'll do. There are perfectly good reasons for not changing, of course, but both represent a barrier between the thought and its expression. Though sometimes we could have been spared that thought—Paul McCartney might have been sitting at a piano when *Ebony and Ivory* came to him, but what if he'd been eating rice and peas, or mixing a chocolate milkshake? Most keys these days are made of plastic anyway, as there's a worldwide shortage of both ebony and ivory.

You really have to try hard to make a piano look interesting. Wild hair usually helps classical pianists make a name, while Elton John was more of a prop comic than a musician during his "flamboyant" seventies' pomp—all big glasses and platform boots. (The time he terrified Iggy Pop by making a surprise appearance on stage dressed in a gorilla suit may be his career highlight.) Keith Emerson used to kick his around and stick knives between the keys to hold them down, making his music better seen than heard. Brian Eno looked as odd as the noises that came out of his early synth, a VCS3, which often didn't even have a keyboard. Rick Wakeman surrounded himself with banks and banks of keyboards, later claiming he used to enjoy a takeout curry behind them during the dull moments (several) while on stage with Yes.

But you just can't show off at a keyboard. It's a functional musical instrument that stays in one place, and attempts to turn it into a posing tool, such as the notorious Keytar of the eighties, just look silly. Guitars are for kids, and brass is for gangs, but the man or woman behind the piano is more often the sensible one, the Gary Barlow of the band, because every musical collective needs such a member. You can be too sensible, of course—these days, a laptop is as likely to be seen on a stage as a piano and that's like watching someone do their accounts.

Fig. 3
*Unfortunately, the 30-minute prog rock keyboard solo had
managed to put even the band to sleep.*

The Impact of Electricity

Electricity transformed music forever. If the orchestral symphonic tradition had been a long struggle to make as much noise as possible, the invention of amplification meant that fewer and fewer people were needed to create the same volume. The ability to record, a long process that took several decades to reach a satisfactory archival state—during the Second World War, the Allies were puzzled as to why German orchestras were playing live after midnight, unaware that the Nazi war machine had perfected magnetic tape—meant that musicians could reach a wider audience than ever before. Combined with radio and later, television, music went from being a performance-based medium, easily created at home, to a passive leisure experience comparable with other contemporary pastimes like watching a football game or going to the movies.

But we all know that. More significantly, electricity actively changed the sounds that made up music. The electric guitar was invented to take on the brass section of the big bands, yet within a couple of decades had effectively rendered them redundant and had created a new musical vocabulary. Its sister, the electric bass, supplanted the double bass, while electric organs could (just about) be transported, unlike those attached to a church. Entirely new instruments, inconceivable without electricity, appeared. Synthesizer pioneers Kraftwerk (which is German for "power station," do you see?) cleverly played with their nation's forbidden nostalgia—1975's album *Radio-Activity* featured an illustration of a Nazi-era radio set on the cover, evoking a promised, yet thankfully undelivered, future. Later the digital sampler would mean that if a sound could be captured, music could be made from it (though most people used it for capturing the souls of good drummers). Technology advances so rapidly that teenagers send each other impenetrable, possibly threatening, messages on cell phones that carry more computing power than was used to send Americans to the Moon.

There were losers, too: who plays the clarinet these days, apart from Woody Allen? And do blind people continue to find employment as piano tuners? But a whole new generation of winners came into existence—to manufacture, maintain, and operate all this new loud stuff. No one had needed a flight case until the airliner had been perfected. It's true that you could just about get away with the human voice and a harmonica but, really, without a light show and some big screens, who's going to pay good money to see that?

Fig. 4
The life of a synth player is always
filled with exuberant joy.

The Geography Effect

The influence of geography on music can never be underestimated. From the obvious (as a cultural melting pot and a port city sited close to where the Mississippi meets the sea, New Orleans was always likely to produce a distinctive musical tradition) to the "so that's why they play accordions in Northern Mexico" (Germans brought them, along with their brewing traditions), it can always offer an answer.

So, Liverpool had ships and sailors, music lovers to a man, who brought back the hottest discs from their travels (which doesn't really explain why we got Mersey Beat and not Marseille Beat).

Fig. 5

Fritz's versions of La Cucaracha *proved popular with the locals.*

Manchester has more students than any other European city, which means that there's long been a ready audience, replenished every few years, to support a nightlife scene. This suits musicians, as plugging away to no one is no fun at all.

In Glasgow it rains a lot, so everyone sits in each other's kitchens, drinking tea and writing songs. This also applies to chilly old Sweden. Sheffield famously had the most striking examples of Brutalist architecture in post-war Britain, and also produced the most significant early synthesizer acts—coincidence? Possibly not. Young men in long coats need somewhere to show them off and what could be better for posing against than angular concrete?

"In a hundred years from now when people want to know what California was like in the sixties, they only have to listen to a single by the Beach Boys," said Karl Bartos of Kraftwerk, and he was right—Brian Wilson's unsettlingly optimistic songs could have come from nowhere else. Similarly, the sounds of the Midlands' heavy industry are often credited by Black Sabbath as an inspiration and a model for the sound of what became heavy metal. In a post-industrial age, quick-witted, verbally impressive music is more likely to come from a huge city where simply getting one's voice heard is a challenge—unsurprisingly, rap was born in New York and, of British cities, only London has produced truly convincing variations. From the famous marijuana fields of Bristol, which inspired the invention of trip-hop by Massive Attack, to the MDMA trees of Ibiza that fed the original wave of Balearic ravers, the influence of geography cannot be ignored by serious music scholars.

Chapter 2
The Genres

Religious Music—
keeping God awake

Music is driven by several impulses—Lust, Greed, Avarice.
All the deadly sins, in fact. But, back in the mists of time,
when people understood *even less* about the world than they
now do, unexpected events weren't explained away as being
due to social media or mass psychosis. Instead of being seen
as the result of an infinite number of interactions, it was
easier to make up an omnipotent, invisible figure prone to
temper tantrums.

Obviously, God—we'll call him/her God here, though he/she
comes in many forms—needs to be praised. There would be
no point forming Earth's first choir to sing, "Why are you
such a rotten guy, God?" For one thing, it's rude, and angry
Gods are likely to do their worst. Also, it's not much fun for
the singers, at least after the initial *frisson* at expressing their
fury. (Later, punk rock would face this problem—most music
genres do to some extent.) Soon it became obvious that
getting God's attention meant that better music was
required, music that had greater value than merely sucking
up to God.

This is effectively the start of the Western musical tradition.
It starts with a prayer, and then becomes entertainment, both
active and passive. Innovations in notation, instrumentation,
and volume would all play a part as the shared experience
of singing together became a major part of religious
celebration, from choral societies to gospel choirs, from
cheerful vicars leading the sing-along to massed monks

a-mumbling. The less gregarious could satisfy their urge to praise loudly at the banks of a church organ.

Clearly, then, the religious impulse drove music for centuries. Without it we wouldn't have had Handel's *Messiah* or Iron Butterfly's *Inna-Gadda-Da-Vida*. Today's musicians are more likely to express doubt than faith and, Nick Cave apart, save the redemption and struggle stuff for their lucrative autobiographies. The line between the secular and profane is ever fuzzier—

as a religious singer on *The Simpsons* moaned after her band left her, "They switched from Christian music to regular pop. All you do is change 'Jesus' to 'baby.'" That's the story of music right there.

Fig. 6
I'm in heaven when I listen to this kid sing.

Classical—
the music of the classes that think they rule

After a few centuries of deity-distracting, it became obvious that music was actually starting to follow some rules. The instrumental palette was becoming standardized. Notation had become an international language. The kings, princes, and dukes who employed musicians and composers had started an early transfer market in talent, which further expanded and spread the word (or note). The top stars were attracted to clubs, I mean courts, in Germany, Austria, and Italy, but other nations boasted talent of their own. Germany's Handel even took English nationality and played out his career there.

But, as time passed, the game changed. With wage bills increasing as bigger orchestras were needed to play the complicated new symphonic arrangements, the interest of the public, in particular the rapidly expanding middle classes, was vital to keep the spectacle going. No longer could top composers rely on a single rich benefactor to keep them afloat. It was now a more populist affair, as orchestras played to ever-bigger crowds in ever-bigger venues. The old four-a-side game, where a string quartet could get together midweek for a session to keep up their sharpness, was relegated to irrelevancy. By the end of the 19th century, the top Austrian outfits, led by Gus Mahler's Vienna, were building up ever-larger squads. Classical looked like it was in trouble, but developments across the Atlantic were to regenerate it.

The lad Thomas Edison (1847–1931) originally intended his recording device as a stenography aid, but other canny scouts spotted its potential and soon it was possible for people everywhere to enjoy the top orchestral outfits and superstar singers in the comfort of their own homes. Fan clubs for the top names grew up all over the world, including the important Asian markets. Yet there were now many alternative sources of entertainment for the traditional classical supporter to enjoy, as cinema, radio, and later television came into being. Soon Beethoven had been accused of rolling over too easily by both Chuck Berry and The Beatles (and, later, the controversially named Electric Light Orchestra). Many of Europe's finest talents had been poached by American outfits, particularly the new Hollywood league, as breakaways threatened European stability. Classical remains popular, of course, but without stars to match the Mozarts, Brahmses, and Liszts, it's unlikely it'll ever dominate musical entertainment the way it once did.

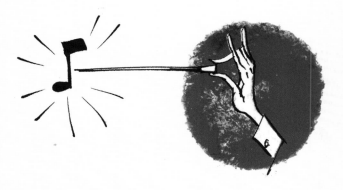

Opera—
the music of dictators

More people know that notorious dictator Adolf Hitler loved
opera than know someone who loves opera. And, just as Freddie
Mercury once told the *NME* that he hoped to popularize ballet
(inspiring the headline "Is This Man A Prat?"), Adi H was a
proselytizer for posh music theater.

"Opera belongs to the people," declared Herr H, who loved to
draw imaginary opera houses in his little notebook, even after
he became a full-time dictator. Apart from the mass murder and
genocide, his long-term plans for Europe involved building lots
and lots of opera houses. To this day, Germany still has 50 or so
state-funded establishments. (Stalin also liked a bit of opera,
but preferred to threaten Europe with the nomenklatura rather
than coloratura.)

When Mozart was knocking out *Die Zauberflöte* ("The Magic
Flute") and *Cosi Fan Tutte* ("Women, eh?") back in the 18th
century, opera was the height of technical sophistication,
combining music, drama, and ostentatious display. Yet some
suggest it had a negative effect beyond promoting obesity in
female singers. During the 19th century, opera dominated
Italian cultural life to the detriment of all other forms—"Music
was opera, drama was opera," complained Lampedusa. Even
artists, choosing food over glory, ditched canvases to paint stage
sets instead. Yet, though there were 600 suitable playhouses in
Italy, no orchestra ever had enough cellists to play the overture
of *Guillaume Tell* as written.

Even people who like opera are ashamed—critic Robert Thicknesse penned a revealing essay which explained that British opera drew in twice the state subsidy its audience justified, and a Parisian opera director admitted privately that his repertoire played to the same 50,000 fans, no matter how many puff pieces ran in *la presse*. Luckily, it was broadcast on the BBC's classical channel Radio 3, so no one would have heard it. Even Pete Townshend, inventor of the rock opera with the impenetrable *Tommy* (which, like all decent opera, at least contains some good tunes) now admits that, as all opera is "nonsense," he just thought, "Why not?" when the idea was suggested.

So, opera fans, you're celebrating an unequal society while living so far in the past you might as well be wearing a merkin, and you expect everyone else to pay. I'm not sure I shouldn't applaud.

Fig. 7
You know, this really would make a great soundtrack to my next invasion.

Folk—
you don't even need a tune for this stuff

Not all music was restricted to stately homes and their inhabitants. Out on the streets, which were paved with dung, a smart lad or lass could tell their tale of woe, or often someone else's, with just the beauty and power of their own voice. Others might spread the word, or tune, and soon you've created a vibrant tradition, where classic ballads turn up in mutations from Tobermory to Tennessee, from Athlone to Adelaide, wherever and whenever Scottish or Irish or Northern English people (basically anyone from the rainier corners of the British Isles) want to get together and sing depressing songs.

The rise of literacy during the 18th century meant that it was possible for hack writers to knock off lyrics on contemporary themes and distribute them faster than you can say "Internet meme." In Bob Dylan's wonderfully unreliable first volume of autobiography, he describes himself as part of this long tradition of singing newsmen. Nothing much has changed in people's lives over the centuries—disappointments, loss, tragedies, and unrequited love remain at their core. Also, just as no surviving folk air celebrates the ownership of a spoon (once the distinguishing sign of a gentleman), no contemporary folkies bother boasting of their new car and flash crib. This means folk music retains its uniquely timeless, blingless values, and you don't have to dress up much to play it.

This air of temporal dislocation is extremely appealing to some, implying both a sense of historical continuity and better times to come. By the post-war period, when everyone who wanted to could go into tertiary education, folk music was the obvious platform for anyone with a faintly left-wing conscience who didn't want to spend too long learning a tricky instrument— even a cappella versions of old songs, or new ones that sounded old, were perfectly acceptable. And, if your family had no history beyond digging ditches for the lord of the manor, then folk songs were everybody's to claim kin with.

In America the folk scene spread from bastions of liberalism, such as cafés in Greenwich Village and Cambridge, Massachusetts, where there really wasn't room to put up a drumkit. In Britain, less wealthy but rich in history, it was easier to plug into the "singers'" scene, led by committed activists like Bert Lloyd and Ewan MacColl. Harry Smith's spellbinding *Anthology of American Folk Music* was a primer to "weird America." Even today it connects straight to a tradition of strangeness. Alan Lomax headed south to record musicians trying to forget their past, and that included old songs. His girlfriend Shirley Collins was in tow, taking notes on every meal she ate—fifties' America was a land of Cockaigne to an English girl on rationing.

That seems centuries ago. But folk lives on, stretching from the "folktronica" of Tunng and the Earlies to the stadium banjo-wielders like Mumford and Sons via the quirkiness of Beth Jeans Houghton, Liz Green, and Cate Le Bon. (With such varied sounds about, it's amazing just how dire Mike Harding's BBC radio show actually was. No wonder he got canned.) Like the poor and, come to think of it, the rich, it will always be with us.

Jazz—
the music of the liberated

No music unites people like jazz. From seniors who've detested it their whole lives to children such as my seven-year-old daughter who is already certain she doesn't like it, its unpopularity transcends age, race, class, body shape. From the terrifying jollity of trad, popular in *fin-de-siècle* New Orleans and fifties' British redbrick universities, to the shameless atonality of free jazz, it comes in so many variations, you're guaranteed to hate at least one.

Its historical importance cannot be denied. Jazz came to prominence alongside the invention of recorded sound, making its stars the first *virtuosi* whose fame was based on their musical abilities rather than their appearance. (The "fat lady" started to become popular in the vocal world around the same time.) It burst out from New Orleans, aka the Crescent City, aka the Big Easy, aka the swamp capital, etc., a place where French influence made certain that Anglo-Saxons were seen as interloping oafs. Cultural elements from Africa (rhythmic complexity, call-and-response structures), Europe (brass instruments, spiffy uniforms), and America (a businesslike approach to profit) combined to create music for dancing that could also be appreciated by folk not so good at dancing, the very definition of popular music. Black Americans might have been forced to live crappy lives, but they sure sounded good.

American criminals, their fortunes inflated by the bizarre government policy that handed them control of the liquor supply, offered patronage to the musically talented. Jazz spread north as talents like Louis Armstrong were hired to play parties held by talents like Al Capone. Jazz was America's music, the first popular form it exported around the world.

Yet the Great Depression fragmented jazz. The big bands rapidly became medium bands. Crooners became the stars rather than an occasional diversion. Octets begat sextets begat quartets begat solo pianists. And, what had once been popular music, turned its back on the mainstream. While the Chitlin Circuit of African-American entertainment nurtured the roots of rock 'n' roll, jazz became introspective and technical, as the brilliant technicians of bebop and cool introduced a new self-consciousness to the music, presumably unaware that in the future they would soundtrack the sale of caffeinated beverages. Jazz became a hyphenate, just as something-Americans proudly declare their lineage, unaware that other humans will only ever see them as gringos or its local translation. Jazz-rock, jazz-funk, Afro-jazz, Celt-jazz, acid-jazz— all are sub-genres whose very names explain themselves and hint that jazz is now a shadow, no more than an added nuance. Still, there's always improvisation, as ever better imagined than experienced.

Fig. 8

Colin's guests suddenly realized they had somewhere else they needed to be, immediately.

Music Theater—
the music of the easily impressed

No other form of music is as instantly divisive as the musical, the lowbrow form of opera that might prefer to be highbrow (that means you, Sondheim), although it's obvious that to make it commercially viable means aiming for the embarrassingly obvious (that means you, Ben Elton). If a new acquaintance announces their love for the genre, you'll instantly know whether you've made a pal. Not many boys sit down with their fathers to enjoy a classic musical.

Every culture has its own variation—the Bollywood trope of tension broken by everyone breaking into a colorful song-and-dance routine is recognized worldwide, though the globe generally says no to Japanese Noh theater. The classic form of a story told through easily assimilated songs dates back to the 19th century, when Gilbert and Sullivan's Savoy operas became hugely popular in both Britain and America, setting a template for many long-forgotten hits to follow.

But with the invention of the talkies the theater could come to the audience. What could be more perfect for the big screen than movies with proper songs in them? *Oklahoma!, On the Town!, South Pacific!, The King and I!,* and *The Sound of Music!*— all packed with Broadway-proven hits. Eventually, the big-budget musical would kill old Hollywood, when the studios belatedly realized that the sort of people who liked them wouldn't park their cars downtown near the movie-houses. But luminous color, decent sound, great visuals, catchy choruses—and all for a few bucks—truly this was commercial art.

You can cover any subject in a musical—singing presidential assassins (Sondheim's *Assassins*), singing cats (Lloyd-Webber's *Cats*), singing, mad, old, posh people (Frankel and Korie's *Grey Gardens*). As long as they're singing, it counts as music theater. This is to distinguish it from real life, where people who sing in public when not wearing Dr Dre's big headphones are rightly ostracized. Even the mad posh ones.

You don't even need to come up with any new material. Jukebox musicals, based on already popular hits, have taken over Theaterland—*Mamma Mia!* (Abba), *Moving Out* (marrying Billy Joel and ballet, at last), and *We Will Rock You* (Queen). Whole genres now form the base of shows such as *Rock of Ages* (classic rock that was never actually popular in Britain) or *Please Kill Me* (the punk-rock experience condensed into some neat choruses and a spot of drug addiction). If it can be imagined, it can be staged.

Fig. 9

Damn dog, that last chorus number in Biggie and Tupac: The Musical *was the shizzle, fo' sho'.*

Easy/MOR—
the music of the economic miracle

The apparent takeover of music by the young didn't mean that
trained musicians, who could read staves and didn't call a minor
seventh "the pretty chord," no longer existed. If anything, there
were more opportunities for silent sidemen called Alan and
Keith, with golf-club memberships and families in the suburbs,
than ever before. Even the buttoned-down BBC got "with it" as
the likes of Lulu, existentialist crooner Scott Walker, and Welsh
satyrist Tom Jones hosted variety shows that required trained
musical personnel who could nail a take in ten minutes.

In America, easy listening captured the *Mad Men* era of high
fidelity and whiskies for lunch. Mitch Miller's epic blandness
gave youth something to oppose, later reflected in internal
conflict at CBS where Miller was a senior A and R exec, one who
turned down Elvis Presley and The Beatles. But Martin Denny's
"exotica," travelogs for the ear, were a perfect seduction
soundtrack for the cutting-age modernist.

Easy was everywhere, from the Eurovision Song Contest, which
replaced continent-wide war with high camp, to the holiday
hymn, songs enjoyed by British tourists on Mediterranean
package holidays, which never sounded quite the same back in
Blighty. Easy was especially popular in Germany, where artists
like James Last (real name Hans Last) and Klaus Wunderlich
(real name Klaus Wunderlich, incredibly) perfected the art of
driving any music imaginable down the middle of the road,
rearranging hits for minimum (or maximum, to some)
offensiveness. (Even more impenetrable is "schlager," a local,

good-time music enjoyed with sausages and beer. When its leading protagonist Heino attempted to sue punk combo Die Toten Hosen for spoofing his famous, purportedly unique ice blond/sunglasses look in a video, the band's many supporters turned up in the public gallery in Heino drag. His case collapsed.)

That the hegemony of rock and pop pushed MOR to the sidelines, yet heard without prejudice the ineffable sadness of Karen Carpenter's voice or the sheer gloom of most Abba singles, is genuinely unsettling. Throw in uncategorizable European voices such as Jacques Brel and Serge Gainsbourg (who actually recorded *L'Histoire de Melody Nelson* in London with the help of several Alans and Keiths), and easy listening looks anything but, as many young fans know. Today, it lives on under various disguises such as "trip-hop," "quiet storm," and "adult contemporary"— all ways of suggesting an attachment to more interesting origins.

Fig. 10
Ah, it's so nice to relax
with some soothing music.

Country—
the music of the quite oppressed

When Southern gentleman Gram Parsons studied at Harvard in the sixties, he introduced his college chums to obscure delicacies such as Buck Owens. That would be the same Buck Owens whose songs were being covered contemporaneously across the Atlantic by well-known Liverpool pop combo The Beatles on their chart-topping albums. Even the white people up North didn't know what their Southern brethren were up to.

The fate of country, like blues, has been closely tied to economics over the years. It doesn't need big bands or expensive equipment. It needs a sad song and someone to believe it. That's true of many genres, of course, so what makes country so special?

The answer to the question—"What culture results when people from a cold, wet place are transplanted somewhere warmer?"—country music is, or was, the music of the poor white stiffs of the Southern states of America. (And, though there have been black country singers over the years, poverty and heat respecting no particular skin tone, even in this millennium, crossover stars Big & Rich delighted in the gimmick of a black rapper calling himself Cowboy Troy after his hat.)

Unsurprisingly for a form derived originally from the folk music of the Celtic fringes of the British Isles, country is big on stories with unhappy endings. And, like their folk cousins, country songs usually have many more verses than chord changes. You don't even have to sing it if the plot is strong

enough, though there have been many great country voices—
when George Jones and Tammy Wynette were married, that
made two in one bedroom.

Yet this emphasis on lyrics means that often the concept
overtakes the actual material. *You're the Reason Our Kids Are
Ugly, I Knew I'd Hit Rock Bottom (When I Woke Up on top of
You), Drop Kick Me Jesus (through the Goalposts of Life), I'd Rather
Hear a Fat Girl Fart Than a Pretty Boy Sing*—these are not only
the stuff of forwarded emails, but some of the most knowing
titles ever recorded, some of them sincerely intended. Perhaps,
inevitably, country music is often the final refuge of white rock
musicians bereft of inspiration or willing to exploit their
patriotism (just as their African-American counterparts often
stoop to jazz in a crisis). I mean, how hard can this stuff be to
play? Not very, but playing it
well is a different
matter.

*"Awww, golly, she's mighty
purdy. She looks just like you, momma."*

Blues—
the music kept alive against its will

The Onion's brilliant headline "Affluent White Man Enjoys, Causes The Blues" sums up the dichotomy facing any historic musical styles separated from their original social context. Blues, the music of the poorest and most downtrodden of Americans, went on to influence country, jazz, rock 'n' roll, and soul, and directly inspired a generation of Englishmen living in the sedate Surrey Delta, including Mick Jagger, Keith Richards, and Eric Clapton. They would go on to add bombast and bluster, and sell it back to America with great success.

It may have been exotic in Britain, but it was hardly more familiar in its homeland. Acoustic blues had never been especially popular, becoming rarities only because they'd sold so few. People supposedly paid Skip James, later covered by Cream, not to sing. The original country blues' collectors were no more than a handful (luckily, because there were so few copies to go round). The harder Chicago electric blues sound was more successful, but it was also less mysterious, with its stinging lead lines, harsh harp solos, and fearsomely masculine vocals.

But it was the mysterious that won out. A 1961 collection of Robert Johnson's recordings would be hugely influential on younger musicians (as was his dying at 27), not least because it sounded like a message from another time, and a place where men did deals with the devil at crossroads in exchange for musical dexterity. Except the skillful Johnson, like most musicians, had aspirations to be successful in this life.

Historian Marybeth Hamilton has pointed out that when Alan Lomax was song-hunting in the Mississippi Delta in the early forties, blues songs in all their down-home crudeness were viewed by many locals not as documents of country hardship but evidence of the blight of increasing urbanization. When Lomax entered an isolated juke joint one night, the room was full of people jitterbugging to a Duke Ellington record. Local jukebox statistics show that Clarksdale, Mississippi, was listening to the same sounds as the rest of the country. By the sixties, when cotton picking was mechanized and much of the population had fled north, the Delta really was the desolate place imagined by record collectors, who now gave it an arguably undeserved prominence in blues' history.

Still, blues isn't solely the domain of aging white guys who need a hobby. There remains an active circuit filling small town civic centers across the Southern states—roomfuls of Bernie Macs escape their wives and continue an old, old tradition.

Fig. 12
"Let me cut you a deal, Bob."

Rock 'n' Roll—
the music of oppressed teenagers

The blues had a baby and they called it rock 'n' roll, according to Muddy Waters. Carl Perkins would later claim to have been present at the confinement in his *Birth of Rock 'n' Roll*. AC/DC believed that the preconditions to there being rock were somehow tied to the racial distribution of schmaltz and blues. It's generally agreed to have broken out of Memphis, home of Elvis and the ancient Greeks, where Sam Phillips ran Sun Records. His label put out local blues talent and started to exploit the rough-edged rockabilly style, which combined elements of country music with raw country blues and a general teenage restlessness (it's been suggested that Presley's access to his mother's prescription slimming pills made him a very welcome visitor to the Sun studio).

Rock 'n' roll already existed, of course. Small African-American combos had been playing tight, danceable music with giveaway titles like *Good Rockin' Tonight* and *Rock Me* for years. DJ Alan Freed started to popularize the phrase in 1951, but he certainly didn't devise it. There's no single answer to the question: "What was the first rock 'n' roll record?" Maybe each listener should choose the first rocking tune they heard. There are plenty.

Its impact on white America in 1955 still reverberates, putting African-American music at the heart of the culture, where it still remains. A wealthy nation enjoying an explosion in consumer options was ripe for rock 'n' roll, the perfect format for television, radio, and the new 45rpm single. Chuck in several million bored teenagers seeking something new and exotic (and in segregated America, black music was exotic), and the music business was transformed overnight. The audiences were bigger, the record sales were bigger, the sums involved were bigger, and the potential for corruption was much bigger (Freed would be jailed for taking money to play records). The early explosion soon faded, rock 'n' roll's original raw appeal superseded by manufactured, unthreatening new stars. Elvis joined the US Army, original innovators Chuck Berry and Jerry Lee Lewis were mired in scandal, Little Richard found God—and would keep misplacing Him for decades to come—while Buddy Holly and Eddie Cochran died young in transport accidents.

But rock 'n' roll had inspired a younger generation globally, particularly in Britain. By the time Creedence Clearwater Revival released *Bad Moon Rising* in 1969, perhaps the first conscious attempt to recapture the original Sun sound—all slapback echo and a handful of major chords— rock had lost its roll and was on the way to world domination, with mixed artistic results.

Fig. 13

Excuse me, ma'am, I seem to have stuck my elbows together with hair gel.

Classic Pop—
the music of boring baby boomers

There's a persistent belief, especially among grumpy older men, that pop music peaked in the sixties, and has been going downhill since the invention of the cheesecloth shirt. They might have a point—rarely have such inventive and forward-thinking singles topped the charts, known and shared by all generations who knew they were living in a Golden Age when The Beatles' latest chart-topper was toppled by the new Stones' chart-topper, and only singing comedian Ken Dodd and singing statue Engelbert Humperdinck ever broke up the fantastic chain of cool hits.

But that isn't strictly true, is it? There's a wonderful frame in John Langford and Carlton Morgan's brilliantly speculative cartoon history *Great Pop Things*, which shows the reality of a sixties' childhood—a mother doing the ironing while listening to the radio, a bored schoolboy wishing he were anywhere else. When we listen to sounds from the era (and to a lesser extent the big, glam-rock bangers of the following decade), we don't visualize sitting at Grandad's and listening to him moan while eating Grandma's stale offering; we see Mick and Brian and John and Paul and Keith and Pete and all the other groovy dudes walking down the King's Road in their finery or driving a Mini into a swimming pool or arm-wrestling with Michael Caine and Oliver Reed. We don't think of longhairs being harassed—or worse—by violent, insecure straights (even though that's the ending of *Easy Rider*); we think of topless ladies wrestling in jell-o to the sound of Jefferson Airplane or Pink Floyd. We don't see Sid James leering or Richard Nixon lying; we see Slade in their mirrored top hats and Marc Bolan (or David Johansen or Steven Tyler) in a feather boa.

There's a great series of compilations called *Chartbusters USA* that contains all the dross and fluff of their time, from Ian Whitcomb's terrible *You Turn Me On* (recorded with the help of Bluesville, Dublin's finest and only blues band) to Van Morrison's great *Brown Eyed Girl*, from Brenton Wood's heartfelt *Gimme Little Sign* to the Newbeats' squawking *Bread and Butter*, hits chosen apparently at random and all with no more meaning than the three minutes it takes to enjoy or endure them. That's the definition of classic pop.

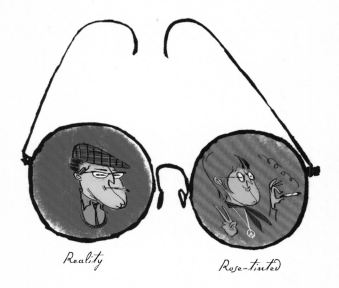

Reality   Rose-tinted

Fig. 14

1960s' life in Liverpool was not quite how he remembered it.

Modern Pop—
the music of those too young
to remember the good stuff (yawn)

Pop music hasn't stopped just because some old men think it's not as good as it used to be. Pop music is after all that which is popular among and aimed at young people, usually those still at school and yet to leave home. But something has changed in the charts, and that's the idea of universality. Once, for a week in the sixties probably, the most successful acts were the best acts, but in today's Balkanized pop world, where even the most recent innovations build directly on their predecessors rather than a wider appreciation of various styles, and several chart hits sound suspiciously like they were put together on the same Garageband app my daughter calls "that music game on your phone," the incentive to appeal to everyone has long gone.

That doesn't mean it never happens, of course. As boy bands like Take That are replaced by man bands like, er, Take That, then there's something reassuring for the elderly. Meanwhile, the kids get Dizzee Rascal declaring that he's bonkers and quite possibly meaning it. Both of them will be played at wedding receptions for the foreseeable future.

Pop music has had some bad moments in the last 30 years, true, but, with the exception of those times when the public's taste for innovation has raced ahead of the music industry (1966–67, 1977–81, 1988–89, I guess), the charts are always full of piffle, tosh, and crapola.

After post-punk and new wave's day-glo glory, it was boring, heterosexual, pantomime act Duran Duran who cleaned up financially during the New Romantic era. Live Aid (1985) reminded us who the stars were, revived the career of pantomime act Queen, and unwittingly launched modern celebrity worship. We had boy bands and talent shows and sexism as a given, and an attempted takeover of the charts by posh lads blessed with undeniable networking skills.

But we also had hip hop taking over, house music rising from below, the DIY explosion of the rave scene, the silliness of Britpop, grunge adding irony to metal, wordy grime, wordless dubstep, Britpop again but whinier, and even electric folkies, yet again. And that was just Britain. America had crunk, cynically patriotic country singers, and factories producing teenage r 'n' b stars, too. In an era when everyone alive has grown up with pop, it simply can't die out, even though it's had several close calls.

Fig. 15

No matter how many times they said pop was dead,
Bieber just kept on coming back for more.

Classic Rock—
the music that refuses to grow up

Like a man growing a beer belly, sixties' pop didn't even notice it was getting flabby. But one day all the good singles were gone. The best stuff was on the albums, and it wasn't three minutes long any more. And it wasn't getting played on jukeboxes, but in hippy hangouts. Cue the invention of free-form radio, where stoned DJs could pop off to the lavvy while a 10-minute Dylan or Dead tune played out. Of course, this was great for a while, but unstoned radio professionals realized that shorter songs meant more space for advertisements on this popular format. You could still hear album tracks and fan favorites, but a formula started to emerge: punchy catchy moments chosen over experimental numbers—more "Money" and fewer "Echoes."

Unlike every other genre mentioned, classic rock is not so much a style as a radio format, one that only reluctantly lets in new material and, by definition, prefers its new releases to sound old. "Oldies" doesn't really cover it—there are no doo-wop favorites here. Classic rock is basically that played with a traditional guitar-bass-drum-vocals line-up, starting with The Stones and Led Zeppelin. AC/DC, who sound like some unholy combination of the two, perhaps define the genre. Guns N' Roses get in, but the Sex Pistols are borderline, despite supplying the Gunners with a sonic template, for their obvious intelligence cannot be trusted. A handful of hits hooks you in for good. Cheap Trick, Boston, and Journey—who knows what lurks in the depths of their back catalogs? As for Audioslave, Buckcherry, and Silvertide, one single was enough. Even Gary Glitter's *Rock 'n' Roll Part 2* still gets played at US sports events, and we all know about Gary...

Classic rock even permits knowing nods. The Darkness have already been inducted, even if it's tricky to sing *falsetto* with a tongue wedged permanently in cheek. Primal Scream's studiedly dumb *Rocks* counts, but their electronic moments have no chance of acceptance. Even relatively arty bands like Howlin' Rain and the amazing White Denim are often tagged "classic rock." Some live on the cusp—Kings of Leon are obviously a shonky indie band; nonetheless, Caleb Followill grunts like a real rocker. (Q. Why does he sing like that? A. His socks are on fire.)

Strangely hip hop revived classic rock. Aerosmith were resurrected following their collaboration with Run DMC, and Led Zep's rhythmic brilliance was recognized by rappers and producers (especially *Kashmir*, a shotgun marriage made official when Jimmy Page and Sean "Puff Daddy" Combs ruined it together on *Come With Me*—the bitches). Is there any genre that stretches so far within such limited parameters? It's a long way from the Allman Brothers to Status Quo...

Fig. 16

Once the crowd realized his socks really were on fire, it was too late.

Soul—
the pop music of the oppressed

Though its origins in r 'n' b and gospel were obvious—its first two great practitioners, Ray Charles and Sam Cooke, represented each tradition—sixties' soul achieved a level of sophistication far beyond its position as mere pop fodder for teens, its arrangements and showmanship influencing musicians to this day.

Famously tagging itself "The Sound of Young America," Motown was a production line, literally and appropriately, for a label that took its name from its base in Detroit: Motortown. Just check the recording dates of those classic records— sometimes backing tracks were recorded years before as owner Berry Gordy and his production staff waited to find the right voice. Based in a rough city where southern white emigrants and southern black emigrants re-fought old battles, Motown made the Henry-Higgins treatment part of the package, putting its hopefuls through charm school and concentrating on presentation. Talent flocked to its doors, not least songwriters, producers, and musicians as brilliant as Smokey Robinson, Holland, Dozier and Holland, Norman Whitfield, and bass maestro James Jamerson (who never changed his strings).

Yet, as the Civil Rights Movement gained pace, black America no longer bothered trying to match whitey. Its culture now demanded acceptance on its own terms. Luckily, this was a golden age of soul music—Southern soul was gritty, harder, and more emotional than Gordy's little symphonies. Stax Records in Memphis, with Booker T. & the MGs as its house band, was at its heart, but also notable were FAME Studios in Muscle Shoals,

Alabama, and later Hi Records in Memphis where Al Green and producer Willie Mitchell kept up the standard into the seventies. Aretha Franklin's breakthrough came when she recorded *I Never Loved A Man* at Muscle Shoals. Just the once, but it set her free from the over-mannered records she'd produced before then.

Soul remains a fan's music. Deep soul, Northern, Chicago, New Orleans are all sub-sets with their own following. And soul continues to appeal. For the Josses and Aimées who've had their moment, it represents an ideal, a blend of showmanship, emotion, and expertise, while singers like Raphael Saadiq and Cee-Lo Green currently carry the torch with pride. Frank Ocean and Janelle Monáe (who dances like a robot from 1984) offer a clue to its future. Keep the faith and all that.

Fig. 17
Motown, where dreams are made.

Before   *After*

Heavy Metal—
the oppressive music of the oppressed
I SAID, THE OPPRESSIVE MUSIC OF THE OPPRESSED!

Metal is the music of the world. From Brazil to Iraq, Indonesia to Scandinavia, Yorkshire to the Yemen, moshers, headbangers, metalheads, and moosehunters are all waiting for Saturday night, dreaming of getting paid and laid and a passing grade. Unlike rap, a largely verbal form and therefore beloved of sociologists who don't play an instrument, metal transcends linguistic barriers through its volume and impenetrability to the uninitiated.

And you need never grow out of it. Fifty-something punks and B-Boys just look silly, yet the aging rocker is as commonplace as a broken-down car in a front yard. No one ever gets too old to rock. Motorhead's Lemmy lives in a little apartment just like any single man of his age, only he medicates with speed and whiskey rather than statins and tamiflu.

Heavy metal can't even be mocked, it's so damned self-aware. Supposedly, Iron Maiden walked out of the London premiere of *This Is Spinal Tap*, claiming it was disrespectful to metal. (In fact, it's disrespectful to entertainment, which is why it's so great.) But now the Tap are invoked as totems of the form. Anvil, The Osbournes, *The Decline of Western Civilization*—dysfunction is celebrated, not berated. Not even the terrible Metallica-do-therapy documentary *Some Kind of Monster* could break the cycle.

Metal, in its myriad forms, has always been influenced by its surroundings, from Black Sabbath, growing up in their

Brummie slums to the sound of the foundries all around, to the passingly popular death-metal genre, devised in the retirement paradise of Florida. Hellholes and cultural deserts are particularly fertile sources, especially if the weather keeps folk indoors.

No reasonable person could keep track of the many and burgeoning sub-genres, from doom (heavy and very, very slow) to thrash (heavy and very, very fast). Metal is a broad church, yet it remains anomalous—it resists consumerism, yet celebrates excess. It glories in power and volume, yet of all contemporary music, its dynamic range—the gap between its loudest and quietest moments—is the greatest. It encourages innovation, but uses a relatively prescriptive instrumental palette. Its adepts hold it above all other forms and value the undeniable virtuosity of its most notable exponents, and it consciously respects its own history. Let's face it: heavy metal is classical music in T-shirts.

Fig. 18
Metal 'til I die!

Singer-Songwriters—
the music of the self-obsessed

By the late sixties, the new pop music had started to take itself very seriously and, worse, was taken very seriously by others. As a new rock press sprang up to gush over the subjects and their work, a whole new level of navel-gazing crept in. Some crept away in search of big subjects to occupy them—the "rock opera" and "concept album" date from this era. Others chose direct conflict with traditionally highbrow musical forms, revealing their classical or jazz training, going "progressive," and often making some terrible music.

But others decided that their public needed to know more, without asking them. The confessional singer-songwriter was born and, my God, how we've suffered. From James Taylor to James Blunt, they've been sucking the joy out of music, and generally sucking ever since. Like most sixties' things, Donovan probably thinks he was the first. Joni Mitchell not only was one, she hung around with others and used that as a source of material, a circle jerk of solipsism. (Her spirit of fun lives on in the works of Laura Marling, talented yet unenticing.)

In his serviceable biography of Paul McCartney, Howard Sounes makes the interesting point that big stars, especially pop musicians who have often been indulged since late adolescence, their every foible acclaimed by interested parties as proof of their genius, frequently mistake self-confidence for strength of character and even talent. Although, just like all the yes-men that surround them, he's too polite to spell it out—he's basically saying they have terrible taste when picking a romantic partner.

So, if that's the case, and we're regaled with songs inspired by the artist's life, the chances of actually giving a damn are not high, unless we implicitly identify with the sentiments expressed. Ever open, the solo John Lennon kept nothing back, even if he persisted in writing songs that mentioned Yoko in the lyrics (that no one ever covers)—the 1970 *Plastic Ono Band* is as good as any Beatles' album. But it's an exception.

The singer-songwriter isn't bad by definition. Tom Waits, the late Warren Zevon, Elvis Costello, Aimee Mann, and even Lou Reed have all produced great work. Neil Young remains Dylan's only peer, as likely to embarrass as delight, but rarely boring. But, as new generations come to the fore—Rufus Wainwright, Jakob Dylan, Ben Taylor, Liam Finn, and Teddy Thompson, to name but a few—things may be out of hand. I mean, what do these children of prosperous bohemians sing about? How Daddy wouldn't let them take up sport?

Fig. 19
'Ere lads, listen to what the missus has just come up with. Gear!

Reggae—
the music of the oppressed

All British people under the age of 50 instinctively move to the sound of reggae and its ancestor ska, so ingrained is it in our pop culture. (For many Americans it's an excuse to do a pitiful attempt at a foreign accent, just as when Ireland is mentioned.) And, like Ireland, Jamaica is a small island of no special importance, but its cultural influence is hugely disproportionate to its size. Both were part of the British Empire, for better or usually worse for hundreds of years. Jamaica effectively had white (sometimes Irish) slaves even before the transatlantic triangle trade in abducted Africans reached its peak—the early drug of sugar inspired cruelty and inhumanity to match any modern-day crime cartel. It's a lovely place, but it's not always a happy one, and, like the society that produced it, the apocalyptic message of roots reggae has always managed to combine beauty and threat in equal measure.

For all the rhetoric about returning to Africa and distaste for the Babylon they lived in, outcast rastafarian musicians often came to an accommodation with the music business. With a Jamaican diaspora spread around the world and a bad-boy image to match any rock 'n' roller's, perhaps it wasn't that surprising that Jamaica would produce the Third World's first undisputed superstar.

Bob Marley was more willing than his partners in the original Wailers line-up to compromise in pursuit of success, letting his record company add white rock solos to his recordings and touring worldwide. But he wasn't the only reggae star. Ska favorite Prince Buster led the way, followed by Desmond Dekker and Jimmy Cliff, as reggae started to take shape, finding favor with disaffected British youths, skinheads, and later punks. White reggae wasn't graceful but held commercial appeal in the hands of The Clash and The Police, while Jamaica continued to pop out hits. The British creation, lovers' rock, as sweet as any soul music, successfully sought an audience of teenage girls, like those who sang it. Also, the Jamaican influence on hip hop cannot be underestimated. Kool Herc, New York's first true DJ, was Jamaican, while talking over riddims—"toasting"—had long been popular there.

Yet reggae came from nowhere. Kevin McDonald's documentary *Marley* featured no sixties' footage of the Wailers even as they topped the local charts, because there simply wasn't any. Even today, when digitally programmed dancehall rules, keeping up with the flood of releases remains a challenge. Unusually, after decades, reggae retains its rebel status.

Fig. 20

When I sang Lively Up Yourself, *this isn't quite what I had in mind.*

Funk—
the dance music of the oppressed

One of the most traduced and abused musical definitions, funk is really all about The One, the first beat of a four-measure bar. Just think of *BOOM! Shake the Room*. For all the loose use of the term—"funky" is used to describe everything from tablecloths to motor cars these days, a long way from its suggested derivation from a Kikongo word meaning body odor and presumably a comment on the physical element of the genre—we all know funky when we hear it.

Inspired by New Orleans rhythms and perfected in the sixties by James Brown, whose band effectively became entirely percussive, guitars and horns offering rhythmic stabs over an irresistible beat, while "The Hardest Working Man In Show Business," Soul Brother Number One, yelped and grunted over the top. (Teenage, African-American, garage-funk bands of the era, none quite as precise as the JB's, used to yell his catchphrase "Get on the good foot!" whenever the funk was flagging, as many lovingly compiled collections of rarities reveal.) Sly Stone made pop out of funk with huge success, while the Meters refined the rhythms even further. But it was George Clinton's P-Funk empire that set the standard for the seventies and beyond.

The funky psychedelia of Funkadelic, possessors of a perfectly descriptive name (why aren't Coldplay called Anthedium?), was beloved of heads and brothers, anyone who preferred outer space to drab life on earth, a long-running theme of black American music there isn't time to dwell on here. Most of the

Mothership's musicians turned up in the equally sprawling Parliament, so named because no one knew what most of them were doing there. P-Funk eventually fueled G-Funk (gangsta funk), Clinton's *Atomic Dog* being the base for Snoop Dogg's *What's My Name*. Funk left its mark on disco too, Kool and the Gang and the Commodores starting out funky before softening up.

Nothing can kill the funk, nor its many spin-offs, ranging from jazz-funk (once innovative, often trite, but usually featuring a good bass player) to punk-funk (where imagination outruns technique), from funk-metal (including the unspeakable Limp Bizkit, the perplexing Primus, and the plain furious Rage Against The Machine) to Go-Go (a Washington DC party soundtrack and quite possibly the funkiest of funk). And you can dance to almost all of it, too.

Fig. 21

Although it wasn't the quickest route, James always made sure his drive home would take him to the bridge.

Punk Rock—
the music of the disgruntled

Later famous as a movie director (and for having an ex-boyfriend called Tony Blair), in 1976 Mary Harron was employed by nascent fanzine *Punk*, which covered New York's knowing if energetic new music scene. Returning to the city after a few weeks in Blighty, she stunned the various consumptives, junkies, and booksellers that made up the Bowery scene by announcing that their artfully studied nihilism was not only taken seriously in Britain, but had become a nationally popular phenomenon.

Due to its small size and unified media, Britain has always absorbed fashions extremely quickly (Sonic Youth and Nirvana would eventually share space on a tour documentary ironically, yet accurately, entitled *1991: The Year Punk Broke*—it took that long to crack the States). But Punk was unique, and uniquely influential. For one thing, it released an entirely fresh stream of talent (that ultimately turned out to be just as dull and smug as the usual well-connected suspects). It restored a genuine sense of physical danger to an evening out, as audiences (and bands, especially the Stranglers, who liked a scrap) waited for the local Nazis to show themselves. And it set free a DIY spirit that lasted for a good two decades, at least until corporate branding became the actual point of entertainment rather than a mere by-product. There were also several great records by bands that either burnt out quickly (The Sex Pistols, X-Ray Spex, Saints, The Adverts), effectively reinvented themselves (The Clash, The Jam, Buzzcocks, Wire), or simply refused to progress (mainly the Ramones).

Plenty of great, innovative American bands managed to leave their mark during and because of punk—Television, Patti Smith Group, Pere Ubu. Blondie were big in America and absolute superstars abroad. But none of them ever changed the wider culture. Yet punk changed Britain, even if the bands didn't sell all that many records. Why? Because if there's one thing Britons of all stripes like, it's a good old moan. And Britons also recognize people who are good at moaning, from Pink Floyd to John Lydon, Victor Meldrew to Auberon Waugh. America is a land of sunny optimists, pregnant with potential. Britain is full of grumpy pessimists, the cup of tea eternally half-empty and going cold. From The Who to the Arctic Monkeys, bands of disgruntled young men playing aggressive, guitar-based music are as British as biscuits and cricket. The Clash's first single *White Riot* is a two-minute apology for not throwing a brick when the brick-throwing opportunity arose. Forget that it took 15 years, it's a miracle that America ever understood punk at all.

Fig. 22

Dear Sir, I am writing to complain about the stereotypical way your publication continues to portray the punk community.

Hip Hop—

the music of the ambitious yet oppressed

Rapper Ice-T (that really is quite a lame name, isn't it, a pun about a tame beverage? But, then again, his real name is Tracy) once posited the theory that Johnny Cash was one of gangsta rap's ancestors, singing as he did about shooting men for amusement, playing shows for prisoners, and generally being something of a badass motherfucker. A good point, although ditties about murder were being written about an hour after Cain and Abel fell out for good. Rap didn't invent storytelling through song; it just removed the singing element.

Fig. 23

JC, original G, according to Ice T.
(See, anyone can be an MC!)

But that in itself was a brilliant move. It is no coincidence that hip hop became the most all-encompassing youth movement since rock 'n' roll. What had started out as a soundtrack for New York block parties—with the realization that with twin decks, two copies, and a switch between them, rhythm breaks could be extended indefinitely—became a virtual lifestyle manual. After the initial novelty period, when advertisers and white rock bands used rap appropriate or not, it didn't just attract fans, it attracted believers. After all, disciples hold to the four tenets of hip hop: DJ'ing, MC'ing, break dancing, and graffiting. Surely anyone should be able to build basic competence in one of those fields.

But it's the mutability of hip hop that makes it a complete form. Accept its parameters—largely vocal—and you can do absolutely anything else with the form. Grating noise, soft jazzy backgrounds, hard funk, heavy metal, spectral beats, daringly complete lifts from old soul records—they're all hip hop. The same applies to subject matter—if it can be said, it can be the subject of a rap. From describing the 'hood and what goes on there—from crime to sex to entertainment—to confronting world problems and proposing solutions. There's love and hate (more hate than love, to be honest), truth and lies, micro and macro, dreams and reality. It's all there.

It's a leap from describing the life you live to the life you want to live and, of course, doing just that can make it come true, if only for a short while. Yet such obsessive consumerism is nothing new—The Beach Boys were describing their lifestyle of cars and girls and endless summer 50 years ago, and that wasn't exactly true either. Brian Wilson even released a song that gave precise directions to his house, the one with a piano in a sandpit full of dog mess (maybe he was seeking a cleaner). Rapping about nefarious activities taking place on the corner of 138th and Grand Concourse isn't that much of a leap...

Indie/Alt—
the music of the depressed

The word "indie" didn't initially refer to a style, but was a description of the record labels involved—unaligned to majors and distributed independently. For every act as effortlessly commercial as The Smiths or New Order, there were literally hundreds of hopefuls with no chance of a play on John Peel, let alone *Top of the Pops*. British indie at least could reach the public—99 per cent of retail outlets were serviced.

In the United States, these figures were reversed. Readers of Michael Azerrad's *Our Band Could Be Your Life*, a history of the unrecognized American prophets who blazed a trail for the commercial success of grunge and alt rock, will remember just how *unpopular* this music was. Black Flag toured endlessly to ever-decreasing crowds, while any danger of achieving commercial success was hampered by the *ad hoc* nature of distribution.

Yet a few years later their successors were selling millions of records, as grunge conquered the United States, and Britpop cleaned up in Britain (financially, that is; it certainly wasn't drug-free). What happened? Well, for American youth it really wasn't a big step from Guns N' Roses to Soundgarden and then Nirvana. As soon as these acts became accessible they became popular, and an entire college-radio industry was built up in their wake. In Britain, major-label marketing techniques were applied to previously unpopular music, and guess what? It sold in large quantities. A few people made a fortune, while many more had a go.

Indie was always record collectors' music, made by people with a wider knowledge than their abilities, often struck by the gap between what they want to hear and what they can create—attempting to cross this can and has yielded exciting results. Obsessive list-maker Kurt Cobain might have loved shambling indie acts like The Raincoats and The Vaselines, but ended up playing to those who'd bullied him at school. He shot himself because he hated his audience, but imagine how much more interesting it would have been if he'd shot his audience.

Ultimately, indie means anything goes, so its default setting is psychedelia. Filter Brian Wilson's experiments through The Flaming Lips, add some random electronica and a touch of unpredictable folkiness, and you'll come up with something like the currently fashionable Animal Collective and Grizzly Bear. Yet timeless, even dated, virtues like crafted songwriting and arranging are still valued. Nineties' indie band Belle and Sebastian set a template still followed by many. Hell, if a band or musician denies being "indie," then that's what they are.

You mean to say we became popular and sold some records this year?
Heaven Knows I'm Miserable Now.

World Music—
the music of everybody else on the planet

A few years ago while on holiday in France, as we drove around the pays, I became obsessed with a radio station called *Nostalgie FM*, which played classic French pop hits and occasionally those in English. (For some reason, all European oldies' stations regularly play Alex Chilton's *Free Again*, possibly due to distant folk memories of liberation from fascist/communist tyranny.) As I became more aware of the back catalog of Michel Polnareff, Françoise Hardy, and, best of all, Nino Ferrer, I realized that I was experiencing nostalgia for *someone else's* past.

I couldn't understand most of the words either, except for Ferrer's brilliant *Les Cornichons*, a list of the best foods for a picnic growled in the style of Ray Charles (Ferrer loved American r 'n' b enough to write the spectacularly insensitive if well-intended *Je Veux Etre Noir*, years before Lou Reed had the same idea). This meant, therefore, that a French oldies' station was World Music, an imprecise and vaguely patronizing term (no one goes out for some "world food"—we eat Italian or Japanese or Peruvian) used by native, usually monoglot English speakers to describe music that is not in English (except the Latin mass.)

This covers most of the nations of the world and, although there's no obvious connection between Japanese J-Pop (or Korean K-Pop) and South African Kwaito (except that they're all recorded using the same computer software), they all share an equal foreignness if you can't understand a word. For anyone uninterested in lyrics, this makes them oddly appealing, not least because one's ears are drawn to the musical details, looking for familiar nuances. (This partly explains the popularity of the desert electric blues of Tiniwaren, which is less of a stretch to Western ears than you might expect from music made by Tuareg nomads.) Matters of vocal timbre and pitching are far more noticeable when there are no silly words to distract you.

Even non-English-speaking countries have their version of world music. What is reggaeton but a Spanglish mutation of several other Caribbean genres (some of which were in Spanish, admittedly)? And what should we make of, say, Amadou & Mariam, a blind Malian couple based in Paris whose global breakthrough record was produced by a peripatetic Frenchman of Spanish lineage? Listening to music with open ears is, as always, the solution.

Fig. 25

Not surprisingly, in Tehran this is just called music.

Stadium Rock—
the music of the indiscriminate

During the 2012 London Olympics the official rock anthem by Devonian pomp-rockers Muse was so drab that while we watched the open-water swimming race in Hyde Park, my sister commented that young sporting hopefuls would be put off competing for fear of hearing it. (Strangely, Muse have recently come up with an excellent unauthorized Bond theme—maybe it's just sport that defies inspiration.)

Anyone who spent any time at the 2012 Olympics heard Coldplay's *Paradise*, the one made up of catchy oohs and aahs rather than anything as coherent as a verse or chorus, at least a thousand times. In its way, it sounded perfectly appropriate for its surroundings, vaguely uplifting, deep, and meaningless, just like the Olympics. Coldplay had truly perfected stadium rock music designed to be heard inside stadiums. The band don't even need to turn up, as their tedious performance at the Paralympics closing ceremony proved.

The practice of staging shows in sports arenas started, like so many later devalued innovations, with The Beatles, when the Fabs ran out into the middle of the diamond at Shea Stadium in 1965 and thrashed their instruments while 60,000 teenage girls couldn't hear or see them. By the early seventies, Led Zeppelin needed stadiums to hold all those adoring dudes on ludes, and the course was set.

Football stadiums weren't even full for football games in the eighties, so other uses for them were needed. As live music added spectacle to sound, a whole new generation of very expansive performers capable of keeping a straight face as they gestured dramatically or ran around a huge stage started to sell out arenas. Kiss needed room for their pyro, Metallica added a grim work ethic, Guns N' Roses used the space to piss off 50,000 punters at a time. U2, Simple Minds, Def Leppard, Prince, Depeche Mode, The Cult, The Cure—the style barely mattered as long as the gestures and showmanship were present, though big, woolly sentiments were never unwelcome. Even veterans David Bowie and the Rolling Stones saw the light (not least because the break-even point on stadium shows was estimated to be 45 per cent of capacity). The Prodigy and Faithless took dance music to arenas, fulfilling KLF's sarcastic self-description as "stadium house."

These days, everyone plays the biggest possible venues, amortizing profit opportunities. But don't forget the strivers who tried to make The Big Music but stayed small—The Waterboys, Then Jericho, even Big Country. Where are you now?

Fig. 26

For me, it's totally about live music. You just can't beat the experience of getting up close and personal with your favorite band.

Dance Music—
the dictatorship of the machine

Let's be clear about this. Some, maybe most, music is designed to be danced to, from waltzes to reels, funky jams to big-band jazz. If it's performed in venues without seats, then that's a clue (though I've had the odd nap on the floor in London's Bush Hall, as gentle folkies have regaled me). No, this sort of dance music is the music of the last two or three decades, the endless mushrooming of new and different sub-genres and advanced by cheap and accessible technology.

If there's one major change in musical appreciation over the last 30 years, it's an appreciation of precision. Watch that Led Zep DVD that appeared a few years back, and even Jimmy Page seems bored by his turgid guitar solos, while seventies' American teens gasp in amazement. Yet John Bonham's titanic beats sound better than ever, reinforced by decades of familiarity through their widespread sampling.

Part of this is due to the MDMA that fueled the first British house wave at the cusp of the eighties—ecstasy makes good music sound great, great music truly unbelievable, but turns the bad and sloppy into torture. If the authorities were serious about eliciting information from terror suspects by forcing music on them, they'd dose them with E and play them eighties' indie records.

The norm became rigid, mechanical, and great for dancing to, but, for all the taxonomic imagination, barely distinguishable from each other. (I still can't get over the concept of IDM— "intelligent dance music," perhaps distinguishing itself from "unintelligent dance music." Unsurprisingly, few rugs were cut to IDM.) The late Ian MacDonald complained about "the small programming differences which give rise to its sub-varieties," perhaps underestimating the desire of young people to mark themselves out from their peers. But when fashions change, all we have is the music. He had a point.

Dance music, though, more so than the other beats culture of hip hop, is omnipresent in our lives. It's quite possible to hear it on waking, all through the day at a workplace, and then when going out to a club or bar in the evening. Has a genre been so associated with work since the blues' holler of the enslaved field hands? Maybe it's an innate response by those who unknowingly miss the regular rhythms of the factories we no longer work in. Even well-rewarded DJs are an attraction because people pay to see them at work. Selecting music is, after all, a process rather than a physical skill, albeit one that requires judgment and knowledge. Yet the very idea of watching a DJ is weird, stalky even. They represent something distant but attainable. There's not a single teenage murder victim these days who isn't described as a budding footballer or DJ, and most of them never had a prayer...

Chapter 3
The Many Genres of Music Lover

The Optimist

Several years ago, in an unexpected, possibly unintentional fit of enthusiasm, an experienced English music writer expressed the viewpoint that every year was, by definition, the best year for music since time began. Why? Because there was all the music that ever existed plus whatever decent offerings had appeared that year, however paltry their number.

One must salute those who believe the best is yet to come and that the thrill of discovery never fades. Even us old folk can remember being of an age when we had yet to hear The Beatles or The Kinks or Otis Redding or The Velvet Underground. All music is new if you've never heard it before and, yes, it really is possible to make discoveries as an adult (I was into my thirties before I discovered the wonderfully warped music of Brazilian psychedelic teenagers Os Mutantes and the impossibly witty stories of Gogol.)

So, Optimists are an important type of music lover because they share their enthusiasm with others. They actively seek out new music, and take advice as well as give it. They don't read about some new iteration of dance music which basically consists of a four-four beat with youths describing the tedious minutiae of their essentially boring lives over it, and shake their heads thinking, "Wow! They really believe they're doing something new." They think, "Wow! I wonder if that's what those kids at the bus stop were listening to on their phones when I walked past" and try to remember what shoes they were wearing.

The Optimist can be any age. Their defining characteristic is the belief that something good and new is going to happen. Many Optimists are those who grew up in fallow times such as the mid-seventies, the eighties, the late nineties, or post-2001, and are determined not to miss out on anything enjoyable or interesting. Now that the cyclical theory of pop such as the eleven-year innovation gap proposed by the late Tony "Mr Manchester" Wilson (1966—Swinging! Groovy!; 1977—Punk!; 1988—Acieeeed!; 1999—er, boy bands sitting on stools singing old Bee Gees tunes) has been superseded, everything goes on simultaneously. So The Optimist need not fear. There will definitely be something decent coming soon.

Fig. 27

I say, these hip hop chaps really are onto something rather marvelous here, old boy.

The Cynic

The Optimist's twisted twin, The Cynic believes that music is so debased that it cannot be redeemed, though it was once perfect, possibly in 17th-century German churches, 19th-century Italy when ice-cream sellers sang arias as they worked, or maybe in Liverpool in 1962 as rock 'n' roll took on a new British accent, which saved it from early obsolescence. All Cynics share a belief that once there was a Golden Age and now it's gone, and we've got to get back to the garden—in historiographic terms: the Tory view. The line between Cynic and Optimist is a fine one, true. Swedish garage rockers The Hives happily admitted that their original aim was to live their lives like those captured in photos on their favorite record covers *at all times*, to the point of actually wearing band uniforms when recording and while eating breakfast.

Cynics aren't merely nostalgic. Nostalgia is essentially optimistic, as well as reverent, a reminder that the music always remains to be appreciated even as circumstances change. Instead cynics are tortured by their own knowledge.

The older Cynic (and they usually are older) will always notice the already familiar bit of a new record, rather than that part which is genuinely original. They can't help it. The knowledge they've built up over years is tormenting them, always reminding them as a snippet of a new chorus sounds like a long-forgotten verse, or a keyboard hook recalls a guitar lick. This must be like the early stages of Alzheimers, where memories are present but can no longer be reliably linked up (and the oldest are the last to go).

So what makes The Cynic so cynical? Was it all those promises of records that were going to change the world and their life that never came to pass? The inevitable realization that a can of worms can only be opened once? (And where the hell does one obtain a can of worms anyway?) Do they have too much *schaden* with their *freude*? Or maybe it's guilt over missing the greatest party that Planet Earth has ever hosted, whenever that was—1969? 1989? 1977? 1829? The rest of us just get on with life, knowing that joys are transient and must be grabbed when the chance arises, and smile when we hear something remotely decent.

Fig. 28

I yearn for the '60s life, everything was so much better then. I wish I could take my iPod and live in London in 1964.

The Eternal Youth

Times change, people change, hairstyles change. Yet some people's music tastes never change. They might have changed their spouse, sports team, even their gender, but they'll still be fixated on that old Bunnymen or Prince record that soundtracked their college years, back when they had hair/potential/hope/a decent credit rating. There's nothing wrong with that, I guess, but, though it might be difficult for folk with adult responsibilities to devote as much time to pure pleasure as they once did, people have continued to make music over the last three decades and some of it has been absolutely splendid. I mean, these middle-aged types aren't sitting at home watching old recordings of Liverpool FC or the Chicago Bears winning trophies back when they could, while doing beer bongs and shoveling down pizza.

Just as a band T-shirt should not be worn by anyone with kids, unless their kids are in the band, it's perfectly reasonable for adults not to care for music made for teenagers. But when their preferred alternative is the music made for their own teenage years, it's hard to win any argument with their spawn about music being better in the old days.

Evil marketeers are well aware of this. The monumental blandness of, say, Coldplay or Adele has proved lucrative because of their undeniable ability to sound just enough like some half-remembered tune from the past, while still satisfying the demands of modern broadcasting, i.e. they sound tempting heard from another room or a passing car, which is how most music is heard these days. Clever, musical self-promoters—the

Cowells and Diddys, for example—have made lucrative careers out of updated versions that retain so much of the original's DNA that zero effort is required to assimilate them.

Yet why settle on the past just because it's easy? Before you know it, you'll be paying money to see some slice of Jennifer Aniston romcomery or watching alleged comedian Michael McIntyre telling an arena full of the half-awake things that they already know. Make an effort, damn it! Watch a subtitled movie or read a classic novel, possibly Russian or French.

Fig. 29

Dad, I'm not going to tell you again, Frankie said "Relax" about 30 years ago,
I think it's about time you listened to him.

The Eternal Youth

The Hoarder

Technology freed the music fan. First we had recorded sound, so music doesn't need to be performed in the moment. Then the radio made it mobile. Soon after, vinyl replaced shellac, and the long player was invented. Record collections came along. The invention of tape, in particular the cassette, made it possible for friends to share their music libraries and for the lovelorn to attempt seduction with "mix tapes." (Or vice versa—I once compiled a tape for a paramour consisting entirely of break-up songs, but she didn't take the hint, even though it included *Part Company* by the Go-Betweens twice). CDs promised better sound and would eventually replace the home-compiled cassette.

Yet it was file sharing that opened the floodgates. For all the arguments that wider exposure of music would increase sales, of course once music became free, few saw the point of paying for a flimsy booklet and a fragile jewel case. And for a certain type of collector the possibilities became irresistible. Napster might have consisted of college kids exchanging the same few megahits, but more selective applications like the much-missed Oink targeted the insatiably curious.

Once upon a time buying an album or two might have been a way of livening up a weekend, the risk of disappointment an important part of the experience—"What?! The *NME* was lying when they called this the greatest human achievement since the Renaissance?!" Such treats were pored over, analyzed even. To this day, I know every word of the first 20 or 30 albums I owned, before I discovered sex and alcohol.

But, if anything is just a click away, legal or not, the temptation is simply too much for us weak-minded bipeds. Like that tune? You'll like this, too, suggests a friendly computer algorithm. Before you know it, your hard drives and distant cloud servers are full of music, so full that you will never possibly find the time to listen to it, even if you stop downloading right now. Even record companies have realized that it's possible to sell records that will never be heard, as old albums, once 35 minutes long, now reappear as multiple disc box sets, artefacts that look good on the shelves. It's nice to know the music's there, of course, but if it's never played, does it even exist?

Fig. 30

Ha! You mean to say you actually paid money for that one record? Idiot.

The Expert

As we move from a knowledge-based economy to a useless-knowledge-based economy, the great specialists become more sought after than ever. Although, to most people, it might seem that knowing absolutely everything there is to know about some superannuated hack band or singer is the very definition of a wasted life, in a world where everyone is so connected that hobbyists in any field can keep in touch across the globe, such obsessive love could one day prove lucrative. Well, mildly profitable.

For a start, choose a subject likely to interest others. Back when I was a till jockey in a bookstore, we sold copious copies of a tedious biography of Nick Drake, simply because it had no competition. The parameters of your chosen subject can catch the eye—if everyone else believes that, say, punk kicked off in 1976 or so, then being an expert on "Punk Rock, 1969–1974" gives The Expert a head start on his peers.

But The Expert is not part of a social club (see The Gang Member). He (and he will be a he unless he was born a he, but changed his mind after doing a lot of research on the matter) is scrupulous about his store of knowledge, the sort of reader who posts corrections to publications that dare to fumble a fact about his fancy. This is serious, not fun.

Taken far enough and The Expert might even claim intellectual respectability. *Mastermind*, the highbrow quiz show (i.e. there are no prizes), now regularly features Experts answering questions on specialty subjects such as "The singles of the

Smiths 1983–1987" and "The Life and Career of Will.i.Am."
In comparison, being in possession of an archive that could
provide the basis of whole issues of *Record Collector* or *Shindig* is
like securing tenure at a decent redbrick university.

The Expert's chosen field is crucial. Pick something as wide and
forever-evolving as, ooh, "reggae" and he will never keep up.
(A fellow writer once admitted that he only listened to country,
hip hop, and metal because he didn't have the time to follow
more.) Northern soul, that sub-set of American sixties' black
music adored by clubbers in the North of England, is no longer
actually made, but continues to be discovered, often by those
such as DJs and dealers with a vested interest in discovering it.
No, The Expert is better off knowing a lot about a little—because
who needs a personality when they can have ultra-arcane
knowledge to match any academic?

Fig. 31

*The markings on this acetate lead me to believe I'm lucky
enough to have in my hand a first pressing of* YMCA.

The Obscurantist

The best letter ever written to, or possibly by, the *NME* (there was a whiff of office in-joke about it) appeared when I was still a schoolboy. In short, it described the habit teenagers once had of writing the names of their favorite bands all over their schoolbags, even going as far as to make up new, exciting, non-existent names just to get one over on their classmates. Inevitably, it ended with the plaintive question: "When are your writers going to throw away their satchels?"

But, not only do music writers love their satchels, usually free promotional items that can hold several equally free vinyl records, the entire business is based on novelty. Being the first to know about something means power, for prescient promoters, publicists, critics, and labels. Though William Goldman's famous maxim, "Nobody knows anything," is just as true of music as cinema, the impression of occult knowledge counts for a lot. The line of command in the music business is so rigid that when a well-known journo was given a boutique label to run, he was instantly deemed a rival and no longer privy to hot tips about new talent, which somewhat stymied his chances of signing anyone decent.

Even among fans, talent spotting has a place. Few artists appear fully formed—maybe The Smiths were the last, and even Johnny Marr had held forth on a weekly yoof show before anyone knew he was a guitar hero. Just about everyone has a murky musical past, whether it's Lady Gaga playing tepid solo jazz in mufti, Florence Welch fumbling with a hippy jazz band, or half of Led Zep having played on half the records made in Swinging London. But the true obscurantist will not only be able to pinpoint the lineage of apparently new talent, they will also hold an opinion on their previous efforts, maybe even material *that its creators do not recall creating*. Frankly, us mere humans cannot compete with such knowledge.

Taken to its logical extreme, *every recording ever made* becomes significant, either as a marker along someone's journey or an interesting forgotten byway. No music is ever truly lost—a rumor of a sunken trove of lost blues 78s once led to a Wisconsin waterway being dredged by eager shellackists, unsuccessfully. But putting it in the right context is crucial. From blues historians fighting over the single remaining copy of an old 78 to dance heads working backward to find the source of a sound, the obscurantist is there to solve the eternal puzzle of music. Well, someone has to.

Fig.32

I think this artist is really going to grow into his sound, but the visceral rawness of his early records will, for me, always be his finest work.

The Amateur Critic

A friend once found himself on stage at a free jazz ritual dropping chains of varying weights into a miked-up wok, alongside a pair of actual musicians he'd met only an hour earlier in a nearby pub. He did his best, but nothing gets past a critic's eagle eye—a review later described the wok player's performance as "tentative."

Being paid to write about music is a genuine dream job for many people. That it often leads to diseases of poverty and alcoholism is irrelevant to non-pros, who simply gasp at the idea of "getting records in the post unbidden," "getting into shows for free," and "meeting people who have their face printed on T-shirts." But those who know nothing of the joys of transcribing an interview with a soon-to-be-forgotten, mumbling junkie imbue such tedium with a glamor it really does not possess. One recording studio or dressing room is much like another, as are many musicians.

The real joy of hackery is in controlling one's own cultural surroundings. Muse, say, might be huge in the real world, but, unless I'm watching an outdoor sports event, they barely impinge on mine. Similarly, if you can't get paid for having opinions, there's no reason why you can't share them for free. It's hardly an exaggeration to describe Adolf Hitler as the most famous opera critic in history (although his other work made him a celebrity). When Adolf wanted to express his views, then they were well and truly expressed, to everyone lucky enough to be present, long into the night. Stalin, too, was given to amateur criticism, albeit more concisely, notoriously scaring a symphony out of the unfortunate Shostakovich.

Nowadays, though, the Internet lets everyone have their say, resulting in such a multiplicity of opinions that it's impossible for a bad album not to have at least one supporter prepared to go public. (In the comedy world, hacks mumble "quote whore" whenever they spot a colleague's favorable *bons mots* plastered over publicity material.)

Crucially, the amateur critic will always pronounce from on high, their views unsullied by commercial considerations or the bribery of a crafty pint with a press officer. Even if they're merely trying to justify that month's download bill, their objectivity is unassailable. The fact that professional critic Y will quite happily slate musician Z on the grounds that Z is a pal of X, who is a well-known dick, is overlooked. As such details will never become quiz questions the amateur critic need never worry about knowing such awfully human trivia. Which is liberating, I guess. Meanwhile, writers envy them, often for having a regular income.

Fig. 33
The performance was classic wok at its finest.

The Weekend Warrior

Most things that are supposedly fun cost a lot these days, even the free things like the smile on a child's face, the purr of a playful kitten, or the sun setting over a tropical seashore. Can we really forget the cost of sending the spawn to college or all the injections that make cat ownership or a tropical vacation practicable? No, nothing is truly free in a world where evil is better remunerated than good.

So the most important thing about pleasure is getting as much of it as you can. Just look at the cost of going to a festival these days—a couple of hundred dollars a ticket, plus at least that again for sustenance over the long weekend, the other necessaries required to tolerate the presence of thousands of other people equally determined to have a time so good they'll barely remember a thing.

Festivals come for all ages and tastes, from the terrifyingly teenage, be it an MTV roadshow for pop fans or grungy old Reading, where most of the greasy punters weren't even alive when St. Kurt Cobain parted his hair with a shotgun, to line-ups of aged rock bands where the real-ale tent is as prominent on the billing as the talent. There are folk fests, dance fests, jam band fests (where running over one's allotted timeslot is actively encouraged), metal fests, extreme metal fests, goth fests, nude-tattooed-and-punctured-people-in-a-desert fests, reggae fests, bhangra fests, and whatever else you can imagine. Even opera.

But the daddy of them all remains Glastonbury. Once a celebration of transgression, these days it's presented as a respectable televized event for the middle-aged and middle class. Yet there's so much going on, it's impossible to catch everything—Glasto is the one festival where a backstage pass is genuinely useful because it provides a shortcut between the biggest stages. The Weekend Warrior accepts that actually seeing anyone perform at Glasto, Bonnaroo, Coachella, or Benicassim is merely a corollary of the real reason for being there: to get wasted and enjoy many discrete occurrences that will all be forgotten within a week. (Incidentally, bands love playing festivals because they imagine all those happy fans buying their product when they get home, though, of course, the punters just have a good wash and go back to work.)

As long as the car is full of drugs worth more than the car, and he or she doesn't visit the trepanning stall, or, scarier still, the jolly posh man who sells *moules et frites* in a dusty clearing, Weekend Warriors will go every year until they finally remember to see their favorite act. If you've got the sex and especially the drugs, you don't really need the rock 'n' roll, do you?

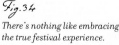
Fig. 34
There's nothing like embracing the true festival experience.

The Blessed with Talent

Beauty can be found in the most unexpected places. Artful camera wielders know how to capture the appeal inherent in the drabbest of post-industrial surroundings. Wonderful poetry can express unspeakable horror. Unattractive bits of unattractive animals become mouthwatering delicacies in the hands of alchemic chefs. Context is everything. That's why some skin blemishes are called "beauty spots" and others are designated "malignant melanomas."

It's even possible to go to a school concert and hear children who can sing in tune or play instruments with impressive precision. Such people are described as "talented," and may not even be aware that they have a gift not possessed by others. A very few such youngsters may be able to generate money from their gifts—it's reckoned that even an averagely successful performer can support an entourage of 10 or 15 hangers-on for over a year.

But the truly Blessed with Talent won't even know how good they are. They'll just sing when they're happy, sad, distracted, or entirely void of emotion. They play for fun, for themselves, for others, for special occasions, and to break up the monotony. They could be superstars or forever unheard, but they aren't doing it for recognition. It's just part of them, like their beauty spots or ingrowing toenails.

Whether they have the incentive to use their gift is moot— plenty of people have got further than their ability warranted due to luck and intelligent direction. If never discovered and undriven by ego, then even the greatest will go unheard, especially if their deepest interests lie beyond music—would Fred Neil or Karen Dalton have been better known had their work ethic outstripped their, er, leisure ethic?

And it really is possible to pass from view. Over the decades, Scott Walker went from teen idol to perplexing avant-gardist recluse. Folk warbler Vashti Bunyan had no idea that her one-off 1970 album had made her a cult figure to post-millennial hippy kids. Living in Detroit unheralded, Sixto Rodriguez was unaware that his *Sugar Man* was an anthem for disaffected South African youth. Bill Fay made two great singer-songwriter albums at the cusp of the sixties, and was welcomed back last year to a world that probably thought he was as dead as Nick Drake. Those who really do have an innate gift do not lose it easily.

Fig. 35
Gene Simmons really did look quite different when he took off all the makeup.

The Management

Imagine a recruitment ad that posts these requirements. Can you intimidate those around you effortlessly? Do you appear to be distracted during business meetings while taking in every tiny detail? Are you prepared to accept collect calls at any time during the day or night from a drummer who's run out of socks and then bollock him for being a big fucking fanny who's very nearly out of the band? Do you understand how the music business works but not how music works? Are you happy with 15 per cent of gross? If the answer to these questions is "yes," then you could make it in Management.

You see, some people adore music and possess talent. Unfortunately, if you want to get on in the music business, it's usually best if that talent is musical. But other skills are needed to keep the whole circus moving. Those lightshows don't erect themselves, those T-shirts don't print themselves, those long-suffering tour managers don't wait on corners hoping to be hired. No, someone has to take responsibility for organization, and it could be you. Also, you get to play with big numbers and are often charged with finding an accountant dishonest enough to fiddle the tax burden, but not dishonest enough to steal from his clients.

Being a manager is more about front than substance. It's about being a facilitator, a barrier between the drab reality of music as a job and the fantasy of success and stardom. It's about playing the part, and really all you have to do is keep the talent alive and not lose all their money (though the late Rob Gretton, manager of Joy Division and New Order, failed pretty abjectly at both of these tasks and is still fondly remembered for his capacity to entertain). The management can care too much. Aerosmith's autobiography, *Walk This Way*, quotes guitarist Joe Perry describing their recently departed manager Tim Collins as a 'sobriety nazi.'

Outside of teaching, where else can you order the talent around, tell them what to wear, balance impossible budgets, and generally tell your charges what they're going to be doing for the foreseeable future. Keep them working and they won't have downtime to spend plotting against you, each other, or the rest of the world. Drive the van, threaten recalcitrant promoters, lie to the record company—and one day you, too, could earn the soubriquet "legendary."

Fig.36
Get on that f***ing bus... NOOOOOOOOWWWWWW!

The Symbiotic Figure

As the old model of the music business dies, or at least mutates, then the peripherally occupied become less essential than ever. Who needs publicists to tell journalists about records when there are no publications to mention them in? Who needs critics to describe music when even the most addled fan can find out what it sounds like for themselves in seconds? As technology literally replaces musicians—just look at the rising number of acts that can comfortably tour, with all their equipment, in a two-seater convertible—who needs a road crew, let alone a drummer? What will happen to the on-tour caterers? The tour-bus drivers? The man who looks quite official but, in fact, carries all the drugs in a neat metal briefcase? With the onset of Twitter and Facebook and the like to provide direct fan-to-turn contact (and to fill up the dull hours of traveling), even the long-established webmaster is eyeing up the possibility of retraining as a teacher. Sometimes it seems like only the knob twiddlers and T-shirt manufacturers will

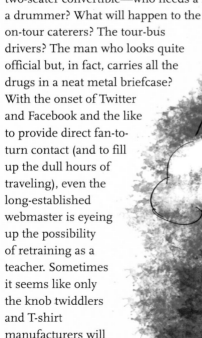

be left standing, and the merch man only gets to hang round with The Management rather than the talent

But some people love music so much that they will lie about it for nothing but the chance to tell others that they're in the music business. That's the harsh truth about being a PR or writer. You get to hang around with pop stars a bit, true, though you probably can't afford to stand them a round if the opportunity presents itself. You'll also build up a good collection of stories to impress the relatives at Christmas, most of whom will be curious about the extent of your apparent poverty.

Nonetheless, there is hope. Such skills may be transferable. Politicians and other corrupt establishment types such as cops and bankers always need people who are prepared to fib straight-faced and can spread a bit of stardust around. Be warned, though—the messenger will be first to get pushed off the boat when the truth escapes, as it will. So no change there then.

Fig. 37
Guys, you're fired. And Rob, you're supposed to be a security guard, so why do you always wear that stupid chef's outfit?

The Gang Member

Some people are experts and take comfort from music because they know so much about it, they can find security in the world of arranged sound. Essentially solitary, they need nothing but the audio. But for others, a love of an artist or a particular sub-genre is a gateway to a social world that will welcome them as an equal simply because of shared tastes.

As well as giving idiots a global voice, social media means that even the most outré preferences can be indulged with fellow enthusiasts all over the world, from anglers who like to catch a specific piscine species to fetishists fascinated by specialty fashions. If you can imagine it, there's some kind of forum discussing it right now. So, The Gang Member's favorite band will have other supporters, no matter how obscure and unappealing their work might seem to the dull, witless majority of the world's population, who have better things to do (like subsisting) than extol the virtues of some impenetrable chillwave/ghost house/post-industrial/ugly metal act, even if they'd heard of them.

Of course, being part of a gang, no matter how small or geographically scattered, is the entire point. We're not talking about collectors of European mispressings, but fans who meet and talk about little else but their shared interest, while showing off the tattoos their workmates never get to see. (Tatts and music are a weird one—one friend made the reasoned decision that having liked The Velvet Underground for 20 years, he could probably risk inking their name onto his arm for good. Yet I also knew a lad who was stuck with long sleeves until everyone on earth had forgotten the existence of eighties art/pop extremists Psychic TV and their attempt at mobilizing a fan club called the Temple ov Psychic Youth, all replete with matching tattooed symbols. Oops.)

Still, for the friendless and single-minded there are far worse sins than loving unexceptional music too deeply. Maybe one day they'll sell their memorabilia and invest in a nice carbon fiber rod. Teach a man to fish and he'll never go hungry...

Fig. 38

I really enjoy the individuality that being a Bowie fan gives me.

The Taxonomist

I keep my records lying in piles, some vertical, some horizontal, some diagonal. That way, the chances of finding something better than I was actually looking for are greatly enhanced. But, apparently, some people alphabeticize their collections, separate them by genre, and even keep them in the sleeves. This strikes me as counterintuitive because Abba will be at the front of most general libraries, ahead of ABC and AC/DC.

Yet the advent of digital storage has changed things. You want to find something? Choose by title, length, artist, number of plays. You want to find anything? Shuffle is your friend.

Some people, though, are just born to categorize. John Mayall's porno collection sadly caught alight before he could bequeath it to a deserving university library, but his obsessive devotion to the blues saw him unearth some serious guitar talent, and also Eric Clapton. The late John Peel, who revolutionized music radio by liking music, not only had the biggest record collection in southeast England but he could even find most of it (even if he couldn't see the floor of his car beneath all the demo tapes he was gifted). Yet it doesn't stop there. Even digitized collections are filed, rather erratically, by musical category. iTunes features some pretty broad churches—Gene Clark, for instance, is tagged as electronica, unusually for a dead country-rock musician. "Alternative" covers even more sins than the evocative "Unclassifiable."

But someone comes up with these names, and they can't all be music journalists in the pub at lunchtime. House, an essentially

Fig. 39

Purple Haze all around, no matter how
often I dust the shelves.

straightforward 4/4 form of dance music already named for a defunct Chicago nightclub, has thrown up seemingly hundreds of sub-genres—to name a few: acid, bassline, hard, happy, funky, progressive, tribal, ghost, and, possibly my favorite, French house, which is also the name of a famous London pub. (A contributor to the Urban Dictionary website rather wonderfully describes this habit as "genrelizing.") The King of Microhouse or Symphonic Black Metal could be your neighbor and you'd never know. Conversely, Michael Jackson was pushing it when he tried to claim sovereignty over "Pop, Rock, and Soul."

Yet without obsessive taxonomists some wonderful music would have been lost forever. The jazz collectors of the thirties, or their fifties' blues counterparts, or the soul obsessives that turned North of England nightclubs into competitive arenas for music geeks must be saluted. Without them we (that's humanity) might have forgotten Robert Johnson, Frank Wilson, or, Heaven forbid, several hundred unreleased Prince outtakes. Music history is happening all around us, all the time. Thank God someone's taking notes.

The Rocker

Rock music might have started off as a signifier of youthful rebellion, but over the decades it's become as formal as a medieval court. Old enemies, like rock 'n' roll and conservatism, have long become allies, especially in places where they once stood opposed, such as the American South. Mods and Rockers no longer gather to scrap, leaving that sort of behavior to equally elderly football hooligans.

But where the old Mod no longer needs to dress sharper than The Boss, elderly rockers revel in the fact that they don't need to wear a uniform to work, largely by wearing the same clothes all the time—work clothes, hardwearing denim, plaid, and leather, stuff that would never pass muster on a golf course or at a tennis club. Rock chicks, too, are easily spotted—long-haired and high-booted as if expecting inclement weather. They know what they like. It's like choosing to eat nothing but fish and chips from age 15 till death.

Rockers fall into two categories: leisure rockers, quite likely to extract as much pleasure from hobbies such as motorbikes and methamphetamine as they do from music; and Lifers, the full-time dreamers who want nothing more than to live the life of a Rock Star. Some even pull this off, often living so large that their peers notice their excesses (such as the addled Steven Adler, who managed to get

Fig. 40

I knew we shouldn't have voted to let the commitee change the dress code.

The Many Genres of Music Lover

himself kicked out of Guns N' Roses for *taking too many drugs*, implausibly). More often they end up grumbling in bars, working in guitar shops, or crewing for bigger names. And a surprisingly large number of musicians end up painting and decorating, the classic cash-in-hand job for those who might need to take time off at short notice if that old record starts climbing the charts in the Far East.

Commonly, they play the part, walking the walk without talking the talk. Not that it's strictly necessary to know one end of a guitar, or "ax," from the other. A pal used to head up to Heathrow airport during his college days with an empty guitar case in hand, hoping to be mistaken for an international rock star. If only he'd bothered to learn to play, he could easily have been a badly dressed millionaire by now.

But the successful are the exceptional. Old Rockers are such universally familiar figures that they now turn up as characters in soap operas and sitcoms, usually easily placated with an offer of some loud and solid sounds. From scary to cuddly in 40 years, much like rock music.

The Elderly Mod

Primarily a British phenomenon and often misunderstood by natives of other nations (some Americans are still convinced that the Mods v. Rockers seaside-resort battles were sparked by a disagreement over whether The Beatles or Stones were "groovier"), the sixties' "modernist" movement has proved surprisingly enduring. Though true Modism lasted only a couple of years, before Swinging London and skinheads combined to leave it outmoded, to this day skinny boys and girls just can't resist a tight-fitting suit or a pop-art minidress. Even the venerable ex-military Parka coat, maybe the first hooded top to be associated with youthful delinquency, still keeps the cold out.

But for every Bradley Wiggins, the Tour de France victor attracted to the style because few things look good on people as weirdly shaped as racing cyclists, there are thousands of plain old Mods, still fetishizing the cut of a long-grown-out-of jacket or a long-sold scooter that would barely haul their middle-aged bulk up the sort of slopes Wiggins rockets along.

Though most often found in the suburbs of southeast England, often cleaning their cars, old Mods do gather in other distant places such as Brooklyn and West LA. Anywhere with live Premiership football and decent secondhand stores will do really. Hell, Barcelona and Moscow probably have an indigenous Mod population by now. And old Mods love to feel themselves connected to the present-day equivalent of what they imagine was Mod past. You can bet there are Sade or Amy Winehouse albums in their collections, signifying sophistication—after all Modernism started as a British recognition that foreign countries often did things better, such as Italian fashion and black American music. And Italian coffee. Americans, more likely to have curly hair and less interested in dressing better than their parents, rarely made good Mods, no matter how much they loved the concept.

Weirdly, old icons of Moddery such as Roger Daltrey and Paul Weller seem essentially ageless, still able to fit into the threads of yesteryear, even as their fans expand, slim only in memory. But that's the difference between an Ace Face and a foot soldier. Only the humble Tommy ever creases his clothes.

Fig. 41
Looks as good on me now as it did 30 years ago.

The Perfectionist

What better way is there to respect the original intention of the artist than by spending an absolute fortune on playback equipment to listen to music rather often written and performed by humans under the influence of cheap narcotics and alcohol on rickety instruments and amplifiers. The history of music is so much the battle of making oneself heard that it accelerated the technology of sound transmission. I found myself in a timeless British coastal town during the Queen's Diamond Jubilee celebrations in 2012, and I can vouch that the entertainment—a flatbed truck of local rustics doing folk songs with the words changed to mention local celebrities—hadn't advanced in sixty years, except it was much louder than in 1952.

Still, the idea of perfect sound is appealing, even if quixotic by definition. For a start, where is the best place to capture a performance? (It certainly isn't behind the drumkit.) The conductor's dais might be better, but, if that's the best seat in the house, where does he go? The DJ listens mainly on headphones, which seriously impedes dancing, while the live front-of-house mixer is always at the mercy of the room's acoustics. Only in the studio can the sound be described as closest to the source, yet plenty of great music has been captured on shoddy gear.

So, assuming he hasn't popped into the Abbey Road studios to hear The Beatles' mash-up album on speakers that cost 80 grand each (no wonder it got good reviews—it sounded fantastic), can Joe Public experience sonic perfection? If you live in a sealed room, away from unexpected noise generators like family, pets, and life, it can be done. The daft and rich could spend literally hundreds of thousands on an amp, speakers, or a turntable with a microscope built-in (me neither), connected by cables costing more than a car, all in the name of perfect reproduction. Your aging ears will be shot by the time you're wealthy enough to afford such a rig, but that's simply another good reason for buying it, right?

The question of sound quality is moot anyway. At the conclusion of Greg Milner's excellent *Perfecting Sound Forever*, an intelligent history of the process of capturing and reproducing sound, he visits a Canadian laboratory devoted to more efficient ways to compress digital information into as little space as possible, often discarding large parts of the original signal. Hi-fi experts are asked to give their opinion, but are never told which version is full fat analog and which are mere digitized skeletons. "It would destroy them if they knew," admits a passing, white-coated boffin. But who needs to know that? As long as the objects look and feel, well, expensive enough, who cares about the sound?

Fig. 42
Look, if you want to listen to the Lion King *soundtrack, you've got to learn to listen to it properly. That means high definition sound and certainly no talking.*

The Lover of Live Performance

"Live is life! Nana nanana!" sang Austria's Opus in 1985. And, looking at them, it was clear that they spent more time performing than being styled—with their mustaches and mullets, they actually looked worse than soccer players of the era. Yet this enduring Europudding of a record genuinely attempted to evoke the communion of the audience and artistes. From Wings' crappy *Rock Show* to World of Twist's excellent *Sons of the Stage*, later made crappy by Liam Gallagher's Beady Eye, that's a hard one to pull off. No wonder notorious Slovenian art pranksters Laibach covered it in a comic, fascist-operatic style (like Queen).

But live performance is what separates the great from the merely talented. It's fascinating, especially when you watch a band at the intimate level. (By the time it reaches stadiums, it becomes spectacle, something different entirely.) Whether it's the fear in a bassist's eyes as the singer glares at him after a mistake during the opening number or the chance of standing next to a genuine movie star in a dingy pub (this actually happened to me—that Nicole-Kidman-lookalike turned out be the real thing), it's unpredictable, every night being potentially different. Recorded music might have lost perceived value in the eyes of the public, but the unrepeatable experience still appeals.

All the hacks might be at the bar comparing notes, but you'll see the regulars in their usual spot. They won't be dancing, they won't even move if an ambulance crew requires access, but they will be nodding thoughtfully, a thin smile of approval sometimes crossing their lips. At larger shows, they know just where to sit for the optimum combination of view and value. They might take the occasional camera-phone shot to prove they were there, but those boxes filled with old wristbands, ticket stubs, and promoters' passes saved at home do the job just as well. They were

Fig. 43

It suddenly dawned on him: he'd stood in this same spot every night for the last 25 years.

there when no one else was, and they'll be there when fashions change again, watching the support bands in case they have potential.

Some concert-goers can even become minor personalities, such as the hippy throwback known as "Jesus," still invading stages in the nineties, or Mr Rat Tail, a big-nosed, small-framed man with a unique coiffure, seemingly omnipresent at London gigs for years. Most prefer the anonymity of simply knowing "I was there!"... until they get the chance to tell you about when they saw REM in a basement or Blur propping up a bill.

The Vicarious Liver

For most musicians, the reality of rock 'n' roll is being loaded into a tour bus, hanging around in recording studios trying to stay straight before being called on to add that crucial fifth overdub or flat harmony, or getting woken up at some stupid hour like 10 a.m. just to do a phone interview with some radio station you've never heard of, in some place you've never heard of either. Exotic it is not, even if you're hugely successful. (ZZ Top once called their stadium crowd "the sea of dudes," which covers it nicely.) In such frustrating circumstances, even a relentlessly mundane drug like cocaine can come to appeal.

But condense the occasional exciting experiences into an easily digestible form, such as a breathless volume of biography or a *Behind the Music* documentary, and you, too, can imagine what it was like to be there when John Lennon's dentist gave the Beatle his first taste of LSD, or Pete Doherty gave some 16-year-old boarding schoolgirl her first armful of heroin.

Even in their pomp, exotic multimillionaires Led Zeppelin chose to hang out with Californian pubescents rather than the Pope or Salman Rushdie, which doesn't exactly make for the stuff of history books. But, excellent music apart, the most widely remembered fact about Zep is that their tour manager assaulted a woman with a fish. Likewise, cruddy plodders like Mötley Crüe are fondly remembered for dying several times (and killing a friend automotively), but not for their limited talent. Aerosmith, the drummer out of Guns N' Roses, Dee Dee Ramone—you're no one if you don't have a book that bears your name and bares your shame. Even the foot soldiers have joined in—Black

Sabbath's roadies*, Keith Richards' drug dealer, groupies like Pamela Des Barres, even aging journalists like Nick Kent and Mick Wall.

So even the sappiest reader can pull out those leather trousers that don't quite fit, crack open a bottle of Jack Daniels, and peruse Keith Richards' recipes for classic English stodge in his bizarrely entertaining autobiography, maybe while enjoying a bowl of warming broth. Leave the boring bits of life to the rock stars, eh.

* It was called *How Black Was My Sabbath*. I've read it, shamefully.

Fig. 44

OMG, Keith likes soup, too. He's such a legend!

The Aging Raver

"You should be dancing, ahhhh," sang the Bee Gees in the hedonistic seventies and, even in an age when strident drugs were popular, they were suggesting that the listener was missing out on something hearing it in the kitchen or car, rather than ordering them to move rhythmically. When did dancing become so regimented that we needed to follow the leader? From line dancing to zumba, you're not losing your inhibitions, you're acquiescing before a threat. Bacchanalia was once spontaneous, wild, unrestrained, marking the end of harvest time as the fermented fruit juice and the fiddles came out. These days, like everything else, it's meant to be doing you good. Bah!

And you can bet that someone will attempt to drag you to your feet and force you to move. Like a pissed aunt at a wedding reception, the aging raver simply can't comprehend that others can enjoy music without waving their arms in the air like they just don't care. "Why aren't you dancing? Don't you *like* music?" they ask, perhaps not understanding that one's sense of hearing is not triggered by physical activity.

But you don't prove you love music by waving imaginary castanets and announcing, "I don't know why, I just love music!" or mistaking the chorus of The Waterboys' *The Whole of the Moon* for profundity and then explaining it to everyone, or standing there looking bemused at a bunch of strumming young folkies around a campfire, wondering why they're not raving to acid house like you used to do outdoors.

It's the oldest and strongest fallacy to beset the music fan—

The Many Genres of Music Lover

believing that the music cares what you think of it. Yet no one, especially the young, cares about The Aging Raver's lame dinosaur groups like Faithless, The Prodigy, Bronski Beat, or KC and the Sunshine Band. Every generation must be free to make its own taste mistakes—they really don't need encouragement. Even scarier are parents who try to relive their hedonistic youth through their offspring. Honestly, trying to stay in touch with what's happening when there's no real reason to do so can put your nearest and dearest off music for life. And who, apart from those with painfully sensitive hearing, wants that?

Fig. 45

Man, these Woody Guthrie tracks are making me come up like a bastard.

The Shed Band Man

It's common to hear the middle-aged regretting that they can't play a musical instrument. Yet they'll take up crown green bowls or Japanese cooking or determined cross-dressing at an advanced age, or equip themselves with a Tour-de-France-ready bicycle decades after their tiny chance of glory has faded forever.

But it's not exactly hard to play a guitar or a keyboard—millions of people do it after all. And, once learned, it never really leaves you. Like riding a bike or swimming breaststroke, you never truly forget how to form the Golden "D," sweetest of all open chords, or to finger that boogie-woogie bass part that you could never utilize when you were in your teenage thrash metal outfit. All over the world, older men (and they are usually men) are gathering in sheds, rec rooms, and even garages, to play music that uses the entire amount of knowledge they had accrued before growing up and stepping away from the instrument. No wonder middle age starts later and later—there are whole bands made up of people who literally play like they did when they were teenagers. And they have a little more time and need a hobby, so they form a shed band.

How can they tell? Well, you know you're in a shed band when your kids are embarrassed to tell their pals what dad gets up to with his friends. And your partner no longer bothers to come to your rare public outings. And you sound a bit like the music you liked when you were young, even though you're not any more. And you can only wear your favorite shirt when performing, the one your partner hates and another reason they don't come. A certain sub-set of shedders can be described as sounding like

The Fall, but not being The Fall (though there are so many ex-members of the long-running Mancunian psychodrama/band that statistically some of them must have ended up in shed bands).

There's something very resigned about such ensembles, larger, older men keeping their dreams of rock and pop stardom alive although they know they aren't even in the same game. Some Shedders even work under the same name they used for their earliest efforts decades previously. You have to love music very deeply to keep trying after all.

Fig. 46
Yeah, babe! Still got it!

The Fashion Plate

Dressing up has always been a key part of pop culture. Entire musical movements have sprung from the plans of fashionistas. Punk rock might have changed the world slightly by proving that teenagers didn't need to practice for 20 years before performing in public, but the Sex Pistols concept was devised by schmutter salesman Malcolm McLaren, who hoped to publicize his boutique "Sex." Roxy Music and David Bowie, two of the most sartorially conscientious acts of the seventies, were well known for providing their fans with an excuse for putting on the glad-rags, no matter how tricky it was to dance in a tuxedo or a pencil skirt. (Regine out of Arcade Fire manages to drum in one, though, which, as the crowd can't see her legs, has to count as putting style above comfort.)

The now peripatetic Johnny Marr makes the rest of every band he joins look like farm laborers. But he simply dresses well, which is unusual for an old rock star, most of whom possess the glamor of a regional daytime television presenter. Yet fashion is not necessarily about style, but about signifying to others that you are aware of fashion and what it means, or at least that you pay someone to do that for you. For a couple of decades now, pop-industry stylists have been scouting street style before sending their charges in front of the television cameras at the weekend.

And, as fashion changes ever faster, its meanings become ever less clear to the uninitiated. It's a long time since the punks fought the mods fought the headbangers fought the rockabillies until the skins turned up and beat them all up. Today, fashion is so detached from any particular youth tribe (save a vague line separating the emos from the soulboys) that anything can be worn in any combination, without representing anything at all. No wonder teenagers so confuse their elders. They don't even know what's going on themselves. Whole trends have risen and fallen without anyone noticing.

Fashion, like music in general, remains a battle between imagination and those who lack it. Hence, crude bling became an effective way for the successful (if characterless) to stand out. Unsurprisingly, the natural step for the entrepreneurial musician is to expand into clothing lines and beyond. From Jay-Z to Liam Gallagher, they're putting their name on it, having recognized that the brand is worth more than the product. But the truly fashionable would never choose to follow a mere musician when there's an entire world to offer inspiration.

The Urban Hipster

What distinguishes The Urban Hipster, the sort of person who believes music bloggers and willingly lines up for a burger served from a Citroën van in the belief that it will be worth the wait, from the rest of us? Well, for one thing, they would never ever use a term as crass as "urban hipster," with its implications of self-consciousness—despite the inescapable fact that, like all of us they will in time lose their asymmetric hair and lithe figures, though they'll probably have to keep wearing glasses.

And, while we live anywhere we can afford, ideally somewhere convenient for work and play, they gather in little enclaves, areas close to, but not cheaper than, city centers such as Hoxton and now Dalston in London, Williamsburg in New York, and Silver Lake in Los Angeles. All these places have one thing in common—once colonized, they then become too expensive for the next generation of Hipsters to inhabit. No wonder they can only afford to ride single-speed bikes and end up in Portland, Oregon, employed in making coffee for each other.

Unlike the conventionally portly, they won't last long in a post-apocalyptic disaster world. Hunting and gathering might be a challenge for those of the tribe that haven't moved up to town from a country estate, and none of them carry enough fat reserves to sustain them in times of famine. Even their futures follow a predestined route, which can easily be researched—the move to a newly fashionable suburb or even some harmless seaside town, kids, a bigger car, and a nagging sense that life has passed them by. Exactly like everyone else then, but in more expensive eyewear.

But the real thing that separates them from the rest of us is a terrifying dedication to making informed decisions about everything, from what music to like to what electronic items to carry to the very stuff of physical sustenance. Such studied artifice is the lifeblood of pop culture, where caring about the unimportant details is very often the difference between success and failure. But making a public display of one's affectations is somehow very, very wrong. These people have devalued irony, a feat that would seem to be impossible by definition.

Fig. 47
Of course, these glasses
aren't for fashion,
I use them so I can see
the newest bands
before you do.

The Dead

There are several plus points to being dead. For one, you'll never have to hear another Elton John song as long as you live, because you don't. And you won't have the crushing yet predictable disappointment of discovering that the new record by Bob Dylan/Radiohead/Morrissey is, in fact, dull rather than the "return to form" promised by giddy critics allowed to hear it just the once. There's no more worrying about playlists and compilations and creating the right atmosphere at parties or banquets or receptions and generally giving the impression of being a man of wealth and taste. No, this is, at last, your time, and if anyone weeps at the appalling selection of music you've specified for your funeral, no one else is going to think it odd.

If there's one time no one can possibly argue with your musical tastes, it's at your memorial service. Please don't waste this opportunity with Robbie Williams' *Angels*, Sinatra's *My Way* rather than Sid Vicious', or *The Wind beneath My Wings* by some pub singer. And, for God's sake, don't use it as a chance to illustrate your life through the music you loved most at certain points of your life—no one wants to hear the first single you ever bought (probably a Christmas record, possibly *Merry Christmas Everyone*, or a novelty hit performed by some cartoon characters, most likely *Sugar Sugar* or *Do the Bartman*), when they could hear what you wish you'd bought (probably *Strawberry Fields Forever* or *God Save the Queen*). And, if you died unfulfilled, why not specify something actively unpleasant? Why shouldn't your nearest and dearest be forced to sit through *Sister Ray* or *Moby Dick*? They never shut up when you wanted to watch the football, did they?

But don't forget to include a touch of religiosity. At my bash I'm having *Bat Macumba, Sympathy for the Devil, Jesus Is Just Alright, You Keep-A Knocking But You Can't Come In*, and *Bohemian Rhapsody*—that should cover everything from animism to Islam, just in case there is an afterlife.

And Rest In Peace from now on. I was having a chat on the old ouija board with Buddy, Jimi, and Amy the other day, and you would not believe the shite they play in heaven...

Fig. 48

Feels like I'm knockin' on heaven's door.

The Dead

Index

Acknowledgments

The publisher would like to thank Lord Dunsby (aka Steve Millington) for his illustrations and contribution to the series. The creative input and sense of humor he adds to the artworks is always greatly appreciated.

About the Author

Steve Jelbert has written about music for several publications including *The Times*, *Independent*, *Guardian*, *Mojo*, *Word*, *Melody Maker*, and *The Quietus*. He made quite a few records in his youth. He lives in East London with his partner and noisy children and enjoys eating, drinking, and sleeping. He does not believe in the inherent superiority of any form of music over another, though it's easier to make jokes about some of them.